Theatre of the Ridiculous

PAJ Books

· · · · · · · · · ·

Bonnie Marranca & Gautam Dasgupta,
Series Editors

Theatre of the Ridiculous

revised & expanded edition

edited by
Bonnie Marranca & Gautam Dasgupta

THE JOHNS HOPKINS UNIVERSITY PRESS
baltimore & london

The Johns Hopkins University Press
2715 North Charles Street
Baltimore, Maryland 21218-4319
The Johns Hopkins Press Ltd., London

Library of Congress Cataloging-in-Publication Data will be found
at the end of this book.
A catalog record for this book is available from the British Library.

ISBN 0-8018-5697-3
ISBN 0-8018-5698-1 (pbk.)

Contents

Gallery of illustrations follows page 92.

[The Ridiculous] is without hope, mercy, history, or any saving sociology or theology. It is a style predicated on absence rather than presence, and as such is suitable for a disintegrating world.
—Kenneth Bernard

At the time of this book's first publication in 1979, the Ridiculous sensibility in the American theatre was already well established in the works of the three representative playwrights—Kenneth Bernard, Charles Ludlam, and Ronald Tavel—whose plays appeared in that edition, together with an Introduction by Bonnie Marranca delineating its vocabulary. *Theatre of the Ridiculous* was the first book issued by the then-fledgling PAJ Publications, and since that time it has entered both the general trade and the university curriculum, attesting to the historic and ongoing interest in this genre in American theatre history as well as in the culture at large. In offering this expanded and revised edition nearly twenty years later, we hope that a new generation of readers will discover the expansive philosophical and artistic intelligence of the Ridiculous in the context of contemporary directions in culture and thought.

Although the antecedents of the Ridiculous can be traced all the way back to Alfred Jarry's Ubu trilogy, its willfully exaggerated style, parodic intent, and irony laced with the grotesque are of a making that is quintessentially American. One need look no further than the daily fare of television, movies, the world of music and music videos, tabloid journalism, fashion, and the cult of celebrity to adduce proof of the

Ridiculous as an abiding mode of perception and iconography in the cultural life of the nation. The Ridiculous was the first American theatre to truly comprehend the American obsession with thinking in images and the transformation of them into a language.

But of course the significance of the Ridiculous ought not to be contained merely within sociological parameters. It was, and continues to remain, preeminently a performative style, blatantly self-conscious in drawing outrageous attention to its theatrical devices and the nature of its artifice. Its embodiment, it is safe to say, lies in the public personae of such contradictory figures as Andy Warhol and Liberace. In the world of theatre, however, the Ridiculous has played to a coterie audience, one knowledgeable about the many historical and contemporaneous cultural forms and images upon whose foundations it erected its wacky edifice. Forever questioning the basis of those foundations, the Ridiculous chose to play havoc with rules, undermining logic and accepted canons of behavior with gleeful, childlike abandon or with equally disarming viciousness. It was play-acting by adults, for adults. But the Ridiculous remained within the realm of art as a force, a "language," still bound by the belief in art as a conveyor of significance in and of itself. Art was to be regarded as a mode of liberation, and popular culture a field of fantasy.

The notion of performance, or "performativity" as it is now increasingly called, has gained ascendancy through the eighties and nineties in cultural studies. Aligned with "postmodernism," it defines in large measure not only contemporary theatrical practice but all manner of cultural expression. It is no surprise, then, that the aesthetics that went into the creation of the Ridiculous—principally its reliance on pastiche, parody, intertextuality, cross-dressing, camp, and its theatrical self-reflexivity—have continued to play a role in contemporary American culture, from popular fare to high art. Even New York City mayor Rudolph Giuliani recently went to a press dinner dressed in drag as Marilyn Monroe.

On the one hand, we have our evening diet of *Hercules* and *Xena: The Warrior Princess*, and on the other, deconstructed versions of the classics. If the unsavory side of sex and gender relations aspires to new lows in *Married with Children* and talk shows, and insinuates itself in just about everything else on the air waves, much of gay and lesbian theatre is given over to "performing gender." Not to mention "performing ethnicities" and other tactical performative maneuvers that are now regularly employed in college classrooms to teach students art, history, anthropology, literature, and science. Even in the visual arts, particularly in photography, the performative is a dominant mode, most conspicuously in the works of Cindy Sherman, Jeff Koons, Matthew Barney, and Nan Goldin, to name but a few. The social, cultural, and sexual issues that the Ridiculous first articulated in the sixties, its recognition of the substitution of image for character and performance for a self, and its unflinching comprehension of the impact of the media on the American psyche are now so pervasive in the culture as to make the Ridiculous seem prophetic.

Given the widespread diffusion of the Ridiculous sensibility in recent decades, the question arises as to how best to organize a revised edition of such an anthology. In this new edition we have decided to include a play by Jack Smith and J. Hoberman's essay on his theatre, to acknowledge Smith's impact on the development of the Ridiculous; we have also added the essays from the "Theatre of the Ridiculous" section which we commissioned specially for publication in *Performing Arts Journal* 7 (Volume III, Number 1) in 1978. All of the material added to the original edition of *Theatre of the Ridiculous* focuses on the sixties and seventies, when the Ridiculous theatre was first formulated and put into practice, and achieved its widest recognition. By staying within the chronological moment of its original impulse, this volume seeks to retain the historical context of the Ridiculous sensibility rather than shift it to the critical ideologies and artistic strategies of a later date, which is not our purpose here, though we are acutely mindful of the changing usage and context of "camp," "queer," and "gay" in performance vocabulary.

While it is true that there are contemporary performances and accompanying theories that reflect the central issues of the Ridiculous, one of the qualities of this theatre is that, though it demythologized art and standards of taste, and demonstrated the interrelationship of sex and power, it still regarded art as a source of pleasure and entertainment, not as social corrective. The Ridiculous is about as politically incorrect as any theatre could be, which is its perverse charm. It may at times be "gay," but that doesn't necessarily make it "queer."

The problematic aspects of the Ridiculous are immediately apparent in the issue of sexuality as it played itself out in the works of the authors included in the volume. Although all four playwrights engage in scatalogical, earthy, sexual/trans-sexual, and Rabelaisian tendencies in their plays, they do so without the excessive theorizing—of identity formation or of gender construction—that adheres to the works of contemporary artists. Even when such work comes close to being in the Ridiculous vein—and I am thinking of some of the offerings of the feminist-lesbian group Split Britches and the work at WOW (Women's One World)—the impetus stems largely from what is, to borrow a phrase from contemporary critical practice, a "gendered position." The fact that critic Kate Davy, in her essay "Fe/Male Impersonation: The Discourse of Camp," saw fit to distinguish the works of lesbian artists such as Lois Weaver and Peggy Shaw from those of Ludlam argues the point.

Related questions of identity politics, appropriation, and cultural critique apply equally to the works of solo performance artists such as Holly Hughes, Karen Finley, and Tim Miller, for instance, as well as female impersonators such as Charles Busch and Ethyl Eichelberger. A troublesome aspect of all this questioning is whether performance today can partake of a style that is not unnecessarily constrained by ideology and sociological determinants. In *The Politics and Poetics of Camp*, a reexamination of camp aesthetics from the contemporary perspective of gender theories, editor Moe Meyer and some of the contributors to that volume attack Susan Sontag for having depoliticized camp and rendered it safe for public consumption by emphasizing its stylistic correlates in her seminal essay from 1964, "Notes on Camp." Camp, in this renewed formulation, is no longer a stylistic, performative, and visual strategy but an adjunct of "queerness." In other words, camp is now viewed as a socio-political discourse, not as a sensibility. Performance is seen in and of itself as a subversive act or intervention within the cultural order. Since camp-as-style was so integral to the plays of the Ridiculous, this contemporary redefinition of it challenges its applicability, unless works are placed squarely within a "queer" matrix and viewed from a "queer" subject position. But, the Ridiculous attitude is not so easily domesticated by "queer" politics. As a truly radical theatre, it defies institutionalized language and values.

If the Ridiculous impulse was fully aware of the interplay of sex and power, self and image and the media, the art it produced still retained a feeling of innocence, a naiveté that left the artists free to address all subject matter and themes and to create hugely entertaining, and at times horrifying, visual spectacles for the stage. Employing a studied frivolity, the Ridiculous was always at the ready to skewer abject sentimentality or denatured civility through a witticism or solecism. Its purpose, however, was not to be an antidote to what it perceived as rampant hypocrisy in the ways of the world. In turning the world and its assumptions on end with unrelenting preposterousness, the Ridiculous neither offered up an alternative universe nor—like the contemporaneous Theatre of the Absurd—hinted at an existential and moral crisis, although in Bernard's case, and at times Tavel's, it came close.

Above all, the Ridiculous sought, through laughter that catches in our throats, a debunking of all mythologies that make this world, in the eyes of the Ridiculous, a place of unremitting insubstantiality. It viewed the world as bereft of all moorings, an ephemeral universe built around illusions and adrift in an ever-expanding black hole of simulacra. Amidst this layering of ruin upon ruin, it embraced all forms of art—high and low, past and present—and all cultures and languages and styles, for to distinguish between them was to acknowledge their inherent truth and substance. In transgressing all categories, the Ridiculous remained true to its belief that there was little else in the world but passing style to cloak the illusions and that its own iconoclastic attitude was but one more illusory style to add to the rest.

Gautam Dasgupta
September, 1997
Saratoga Springs, New York

Introduction to the 1979 Edition

bonnie marranca

The Ridiculous has been a definable sensibility in the American theatre for more than a dozen years now. It never had a manifesto or any official theories—the formal, self-conscious documents that sometimes announce a radical movement in art—but evolved rather informally on its own in the mid-sixties. Jack Smith, whose radically innovative and personal films (*Flaming Creatures, Normal Love*) had a profound influence on the development of the Ridiculous approach to art, is acknowledged as the father of the style.

But in theatre the Ridiculous aesthetic has come to be identified with the playwrights Kenneth Bernard, Charles Ludlam, and Ronald Tavel, and director John Vaccaro who, at one time or another, directed plays by each of them. An interesting note: Tavel's *The Life of Lady Godiva*, which John Vaccaro directed in its 1966 premiere, featured a young Charles Ludlam in the cast. It was the first staging under the banner of The Play-House of the Ridiculous, though not the earliest of the "Ridiculous" productions. Kenneth Bernard didn't begin working with Vaccaro until 1968 (Tavel and Vaccaro split in 1967), the year after Ludlam founded The Ridiculous Theatrical Company.

What happened in the years that followed the initial coalition of the Ridiculous around certain artists and attitudes imitates the random logic of creativity. Like most independent discoveries of style, its historical course is less discernible than the consciousness in the artworks themselves.

What is the Ridiculous? Here's one way to describe it: an anarchic undermining of political, sexual, psychological, and cultural categories, frequently in dramatic structures that parody classical literary forms or re-function American popular entertainments, and always allude to themselves as "performances." A highly self-conscious style, the Ridiculous tends toward camp, kitsch, transvestism, the grotesque, flamboyant visuals, and literary dandyism. It is comedy beyond the absurd because it is less intellectual, more earthy, primal, liberated. Not tragicomedy but metaphysical burlesque, the Ridiculous offers a new version of the "clown." Its dependency on the icons, artifacts, and entertainments of mass culture in America—the "stars," old movies, popular songs, television, and advertising—makes the Ridiculous a truly indigenous American approach to making theatre.

Who is the Ridiculous? There is a long list of people who touch base with this style since it has spread over the years from film and theatre into the worlds of television, rock music, and fashion. Here is a start: Jeff Weiss, Rochelle Owens, H. M. Koutoukas, Hot Peaches, "The Gong Show" celebrities, Rosalyn Drexler, Tom Eyen, Jackie Curtis, Seth Allen, Christopher Durang, Albert Innaurato, Harvey Fierstein, Tom O'Horgan, Divine, Alice Cooper, punk rockers, Bette Midler, John Waters. And, of course, Kenneth Bernard, Charles Ludlam, Ronald Tavel.

• • •

The original program for Ronald Tavel's *The Life of Lady Godiva* states, "We have passed beyond the absurd; our situation is absolutely preposterous." One look at *Lady Godiva* will prove it. The play takes as its starting point the eleventh-century legendary figure, and in a structure that parodies medieval and Elizabethan literary convention, cowboy and grade-B movies, Tavel brings together references to television, the *New York Post*, the Rockettes, Franz Liszt, and Art Nouveau in one campy, anachronistic whole. No wonder he subtitled the play "an hysterical drama."

In *Lady Godiva* Tavel turns a tale of sex, mistaken identity, and mock religious fervor—in a convent doubling as a brothel—into "the hysterical adventures of Coventry Convent." The opening words of the play are, "You will discover that from this point on, every line is better than the next." And indeed Tavel does his best to provide us with his characteristic puns, aphoristic sayings, and wisecrack comments on the festivities. "Nudity is the quintessence of essence, though it is sick-rilegious to say so."

Mother Superviva (in drag) leads the blasphemous party; assisting her are Godiva (in Gibson Girl dress, sometimes speaking in a Brooklyn accent), Peeping Tom, Sister Kasha Veronicas (the convent's cobbler), Superviva's sheriff son Thorold, and Leofric, a Warwickshire Lord in S & M garb. All of these characters work to undercut literary, psychological, social, and sexual categories, and offer in their stead a burlesque of tacky splendor.

Lady Godiva features many of the staples of Ridiculous theatre: sexual exuberance and transvestism, the mix-and-match of "high" and "low" culture, camp, visual flamboyance, and comic humiliation of respectable figures. *Lady Godiva* insists on having fun with itself, and Tavel always seems to be winking at his audience.

The characters in the play often refer to their roles in a "performance." At one point Tom announces: "this is the divertissement: it has nothing to do with the rest of the play. . . . Its purpose is to give the other actors time to change costumes." Sister Veronicas has a marvelous line that simultaneously mocks the inanities of television commercials and offers a visual pun on a rape scene that she covers with a screen: "We'll ban this scene to take the worry out of being close." *Lady Godiva* abounds in this sort of wordplay, but in this instance Tavel offers a little more—an advertising twist plus a "classical" screen scene.

Lady Godiva is hardly meant to teach history, so it is no wonder we never get to see Godiva take her famous ride. But it's fun to watch a chorus of nuns urge her on with a Rockettes routine. There are jokes in purposely "bad" taste (it's so bad it's good) and puns to make you groan, but Tavel does manage to sprinkle sound opinions among the more raunchy ones: "Words are an art form. Stop trying to use them to communicate with."

Lady Godiva is the campy, sexually playful side of the Ridiculous. Not only does it illustrate the Ridiculous's grounding in popular culture (in this period of his career, Tavel is the American theatre's pop artist par excellence), but even more important, its dependence on performance to realize itself. *The Life of Lady Godiva* is art about artifice.

●　●　●

Charles Ludlam's *Stage Blood* is an example of the literary side of the Ridiculous. Though *The Life of Lady Godiva* and *The Magic Show of Dr. Magico* make use of literary figures, *Stage Blood* is the play that makes the most specific literary reference—in this case, to Shakespeare's *Hamlet.*

What Ludlam has done is to create a backstage comedy of murder and intrigue to run parallel to the production of *Hamlet* which a certain Caucasian Theatrical Company is performing in the town of Mudville. In Ludlam's sense of the Ridiculous—closer to Tavel than Bernard—the classical text is merely the jumping-off point or the pretext for another kind of dramatic experience. As often happens in the Ridiculous, the classical form enters into a dialogue with the new form.

The backstage *Hamlet* is far more complicated plot-wise than Shakespeare's play because Ludlam turns everything upside down. Using only the structural similarities of *Hamlet,* he devises not a variation on the metaphysical quest theme, but a Shakespearean-style whodunit.

In *Stage Blood* Ludlam mixes Shakespeare, the clichés of backstage film comedies, the conventions and stock characters of nineteenth-century melodrama, and his own brand of Elizabethan versifying to fashion a play in the grand old style that he so obviously loves. In the process he takes the opportunity to offer his interpretation of *Hamlet* ("*Hamlet* gave to the mystery story the one quality it had formerly lacked . . . a streak of the irrational"), spoof the pretensions of experimental theatre ("If Grotowski calls his book 'Towards a Poor Theater,' why does the book cost fifteen dollars?"), and comment on the art of acting ("What do you know of honesty and truth? I call it lies and deception.").

An ode to the joy of making theatre, *Stage Blood* is a witty example of the parodistic approach to Western cultural tradition that is behind the Ridiculous aesthetic. Ludlam obviously loves the theatrical past of grand gestures and eloquent speech, but rather than turn it into museum theatre he takes the tradition and filters it through a liberated consciousness to make it his own. A certain sense of nostalgia for the great age of acting prevails in *Stage Blood*, but there is a good deal of self-conscious "in" joking, too.

The offhand casualness of the dialogue and the campy sense of performance carry *Stage Blood* beyond comedy into the Ridiculous. Attitude more than anything else defines this style of theatre. It is the free-spirited use of his materials, the willingness for comedy to go beyond laughter, for the text to go beyond dramatic literature, and for the characters to approach archetypes that place Ludlam in the realm of the Ridiculous. In *Stage Blood* it is not necessary to suspend your disbelief because this *Hamlet* within a *Hamlet* proves that life imitates art—in strange ways.

* * * *

The grotesque side of the Ridiculous is reflected in Kenneth Bernard's *The Magic Show of Dr. Ma-Gico*. Set in a seventeenth-century drawing room bordered by mirrors, the play is a series of episodes orchestrated by the magician Ma-Gico for the "enlightenment" of his audience (in the play and in the theatre). But the illusionist's "lessons" are bitter illustrations of disillusionment. "I do not deal in tricks . . . *I* deal in life," he cautions.

Bernard's plays are characterized by a nightmarish vision of society and this one is no exception. In the manner of Grand Guignol, *Dr. Ma-Gico* counterpoints gavottes and minuets, magic tricks, sounds of harpsichord, recorder, and flute, with scenes of violence and eroticism in a cabaret revue of romance and intrigue, under the direction of its demonic master of ceremonies.

Through a succession of "turns" on the themes of evil, justice, and betrayal, *Dr. Ma-Gico* invites the spectator—or is he a voyeur?—into a reflecting world of violent images, peopled by royalty, courtiers, and commoners. Ma-Gico himself is the narrator and actor in his theatre; the grand illusionist, he teaches by negative example. But what is the lesson to be learned?

Central to this theatre is the figure of a King who appears in various settings in several of the magic show's eight episodes. A symbol of authority and power, he is humiliated and his sense of justice perverted. But there is no justice in the world of Ma-Gico: a young woman castrates her lover to "test" him, a Queen dies from the orgasmic overzealousness of her King, even a fairy tale turns to tragedy when a young Prince kills his lover by mistake. *Dr. Ma-Gico* unfolds as a succession of ironic reversals.

Complementing the perverse erotics of his characters are the horrific images (mostly sexual) Bernard conjures up for his brand of the Ridiculous—a young man's huge erection after he is hanged, the bloody stump of a penis hanging from the mouth of a young woman who has just castrated her lover. *Dr. Ma-Gico* evolves through sexual grotesques, set against a background of elegant courtliness.

In Bernard's conception of the Ridiculous the world is a place of sexual perversion and betrayal; human contact at a normative level is impossible in this living hell. The reflecting mirrors keep throwing the distorted images of the theatrical caricatures back to us, and we in turn are reflected in the all-seeing, all-distorting eye of the "world." Bernard is the dark spirit of the Ridiculous, and *The Magic Show of Dr. Ma-Gico* one of his bleakest plays.

* * *

Each of the playwrights in this volume comes to the Ridiculous from a different angle, as the plays amply demonstrate. And though the texts can be read as texts, it is only in the theatre that the Ridiculous can be fully realized. It is a *performance style* above all else. Here, then, are three approaches to the aesthetics of the Ridiculous.

Bonnie Marranca
November 1978
New York City

Theatre of the Ridiculous

The Theatre of Jack Smith

j. hoberman

From the mid-1960s on, Jack Smith—best-known as the director of *Flaming Creatures* (1962–63), a key work in the American avant-garde film—has astonished New York audiences with a series of highly influential performance pieces. Although Smith's theatre, which is even more fugitive and underground than his film production, has attracted little critical writing, it has made itself felt in the work of artists as otherwise disparate as Ronald Tavel, John Vaccaro, Richard Foreman, and Robert Wilson. At the same time, Smith's refusal to separate his persona from his art presaged the gallery-based "performance artists" of the mid-1970s. His presentations include the ongoing slide-show (known variously as *Spiritual Oasis of Lucky Landlord Paradise, Fear Ritual of Shark Museum, Horror of the Rented World*), which has in some ways superseded his 16mm film work, and a number of individual plays. Both modes are original and important contributions to American art.

Born in Columbus, Ohio, in 1932, Smith was closely associated in the late 1950s with the filmmaker Ken Jacobs, appearing in Jacobs' *Little Stabs at Happiness* (1958–61) and the unfinished *Star Spangled to Death* (1957–). *Blonde Cobra* (1959–62), which Jacobs edited from footage shot by Bob Flieschner, is a portrait of Smith. During the sum-

Originally published in *The Drama Review* 23, no. 1 (March 1979). Reprinted with permission. Jack Smith died in 1989.

mer of 1961, Smith and Jacobs went to Provincetown, where they opened a nightclub show, *The Human Wreckage Review*. The show was soon shut down by the police, who objected to a blasphemous reference to the pope. In a small way, this censorship foreshadowed the cause célèbre of Smith's *Flaming Creatures*. The film's use of male and female nudity caused it to be taken to trial and eventually banned in the state of New York. Today, Smith is extremely bitter that this film, "designed as a comedy," was turned into "a sex issue of the Cocktail World."

Smith's subsequent films included *Normal Love* (1964) and *No President* (1969), and he appeared in those of Andy Warhol, Ron Rice, George Kuchar, Gregory Markopolous, and other New York City underground filmmakers. As with Orson Welles in the commercial cinema, Smith-the-actor's strong artistic personality exerted a decisive influence, not only in his own scenes, but often over the entire film. With the decline of an actor-oriented, avant-garde cinema, he increasingly appeared in live performances. These included his own works, the Ridiculous Theatre's *Big Hotel* (1967), and Robert Wilson's *Life and Times of Sigmund Freud* (1971).

Smith considers his first major theatre piece to be *Destruction of Atlantis*, which was performed twice in November 1965 as part of the "New Cinema Festival." The production was briefly described by Jonas Mekas in the *Village Voice* as "an orgy of costumes, suppressed and open violence, and color (whose center) was a huge red lobster, a masterpiece creation of costume and character." Smith's script was later published in *Film Culture* #40.

The play, set in "a child's vegetable garden of foreign policy cadavers," appears to have been a long, loosely linked, and extravagant series of events, including dance, film, and tape. According to Smith's script, the spectators file into the theatre blindfolded, and are harangued over the public address system by a "mad voice":

> You are to imagine that you are a wino. This afternoon you were overcome by a fit of drowsiness and you slumped to the sidewalk. You lie there in the sun—baking and half asleep. Your skin feels oily. Your socks

are clammy. Your head feels like a coconut—your eyes like sore rectums. You are uncomfortably hot but you lie entirely motionless. A police wino wagon drives up and suddenly, rudely, you are prodded by a nightstick. You are dragged to your feet. You had a bottle in your pocket that was deliberately smashed by the nightstick. All the way to the police station you have to sit on a pocketful of broken glass with a wet pant leg. You are driven to a skyscraper prison. It is disguised to look like an ordinary skyscraper.

The curtains then open on "the Siamese (North and South) twin queens of Atlantis," who inform the audience that they might now remove their blindfolds. The twins decide to smoke marijuana, and their slave-girl Mehboubeh brings them a pipe. However, the twins must leave the stage in search of matches. On their return, a procession of dancers enters "and film is projected over them for a production number illustrating the tawdry waste of wealthy mfgrs."

Eventually the twins quarrel over the central arm of their armchair-throne and "end by dragging it clumsily offstage." At this point the lobster makes his entrance, "with gigantic salad fork and spoon and crepe paper lettuce leaves." The twins reappear and are arrested by the "U.S. federal narcos in rat masks" who have been continually lurking in the background. Taken to an operating table, the twins are "severed with an electric circular saw," as Mario Montez dances around them to the music from *Swan Lake*. They die and the lobster covers their bodies with lettuce. He collects everything onstage into a pile. Smoke ("as from a volcano") rises to obscure him and he ends the play by screaming at the audience: "Put back your blindfolds—then don't—I don't care—get out I don't need you—Get out of my dressing room—out!!"

Destruction of Atlantis displayed many characteristics of Smith's later performances: the privileged position of the audience is rendered problematic; political content is couched in terms of Hollywood exotica; found material, such as the display of a *National Enquirer* headline—"Mother Kills Twin So Other May Live" (cited in the script), figures prominently. According to Mekas's review, the piece "relied on chance, on coincidence, on conglomerations." Others who were present remember its slow, hypnotic pacing and rich atmosphere of confusion. It is re-called that the twins had particular difficulty in coordinating their move-ments. As they had many entrances and exits, this "problem" was prob-ably contrived by Smith. "I don't ask people to act," he told an interviewer several years later. "It should be more like reacting to stimuli."

The sense of theatre as a constantly breaking-down ritual/re-hearsal was further developed in Smith's next series of pieces. From the spring of 1970 until his eviction two years later, he staged midnight performances at The Plaster Foundation of Atlantis, a duplex loft in Low-er Manhattan. These pieces were located in what Robert Rauschenberg once called "the gap between art and life." The Plaster Foundation was both Smith's home and his theatre, and the spectator often had the feeling that what one saw enacted there was no more or less than Smith's daily existence, framed by an audience's presence. The spec-tacle began with one's arrival and ended several hours later when Smith disappeared into his loft's upper reaches.

Half of the loft's middle ceiling had been removed. The remain-ing portion sheltered a collection of old chairs and sofas—eventually a rickety wooden grandstand—for the audience. At the center of the loft was the performance area, a fantastic accumulation of refuse and junk. This assemblage surrounded a simulated lagoon, made from an inflat-able pool, with plastic tubing providing a small waterfall. Farther back was an upright victrola, encased in a coffin, from which issued a steady selection of scratchy Latin, Hawaiian, and exotic mood music, Holly-wood scores, occasional pop songs, or educational records. Behind this a few flats stood propped against each other to create a murky backstage area.

The set demonstrated Smith's assertion (in his 1962 text, "The Perfect Film Appositeness of Maria Montez") that "trash is the material of creators." Like Kurt Schwitters' legendary *merzbau*, Smith's monu-mental assemblage was both specific to its location and continually growing. It incorporated all manner of material, much of which must have been found on the streets of the still-industrial neighborhood where The Plaster Foundation was located. Included were empty bot-

J. Hoberman

tles and tin cans, old magazines and fallen pieces of plaster, a toilet, crutches, a number of commercial signs ("Free All Day," "U.S. Gypsum"), a large heart-shaped candy box and several dried-out Christmas trees, feathers and streamers, a rubber dinosaur, a teddy bear, various dolls and parts of mannequins. The assemblage was festooned with Christmas tinsel, glitter, and birthday candles, and bathed by colored theatre lights from above. Smith encouraged contemplation of his set's structure by spending a minimum of thirty to forty minutes of each performance making minor adjustments in its composition, or pretending to vacuum it while wrapped in a shawl.

Several images that Smith, in a 1978 interview with Sylvère Lotringer, employed to outline his ideas for an improved society, inescapably bring The Plaster Foundation to mind:

> In the middle of the city should be a repository of objects that people don't want anymore, which they would take to this giant junkyard. . . . This center of unused objects would become a center of intellectual activity. Things would grow up around it.

And in describing an ideal house:

> Everything to do with water would be in one place, and it would be in the form of a waterfall; and it would be enclosed, and plants would be happy there; washing the dishes would become a Polynesian thing.

The Plaster Foundation's play, which varied wildly from performance to performance, involved, in a general sense, listening to music, waiting for the performers to finish dressing up, and watching the slow burial and exhumation of artifacts from the set. It was performed under a number of titles, including *Withdrawal from Orchid Lagoon*, *Spiritual Oasis of Lucky Landlord Paradise*, and *Economic and Religious Spectacle of Jingola*. The cast, usually referred to as the Reptilian Theatrical Company, also varied and Smith occasionally performed alone. On those nights when there were actors, much of the performance revolved around their preparations. They often appeared to be unrehearsed and/or confused, reading from the script whose pages were passed around the stage. Almost always Smith gave them cues and direction while they were performing. With wonderful understatement, a 1971 press release for Smith's never-produced *Hamlet and the 1001 Psychological Jingoleanisms of Prehistoric Rima-Puu* cites The Plaster Foundation as "an experimental free theatre" whose major discovery was "the realization that thinking is interesting onstage."

The evocative music, the lateness of the hour, the slowness of the action, the joints that occasionally circulated through the small (and serious) audience combined to create an elastic framework that successfully encompassed all mishaps and delays—in fact, anything that happened—into the framework of Smith's art. Some of the performance's recurring themes, as well as its pervasive sense of entropy, decay, and collapse, were anticipated by *The Memoirs of Maria Montez*, a text Smith published in 1963:

> Maria Montez was propped up beside the pool which reflected her ravishing beauty. A chunk fell off her face showing the grey underneath her rouge. . . . Any clever character actor could play the makeup woman in chinese drag. We need all the character actresses to impersonate the staff which doesn't exist. . . . We will go on with this scene; we'll just pretend it's a sirocco scene and just restore Miss Montez's face. We'll have to use what's left of her leg because some of her face got stepped on. I'll put her in a voluminous cloak that will show only her face. The leading man can have his head buried in a chunk of her hair. That'll prop him up. . . . The love scene by the pool is finally being shot. There's no indication that the camera is working though. But if we had to worry about that we'd go mad. Well I'm the only one here.

Although some performances at the Plaster Foundation had an unmistakable aura of menace, others were lighter and more relaxed, characterized by the ironic juxtaposition of music and activity and Smith's deadpan clowning.

The fullest contemporary account of one of these evenings is Jonas Mekas's subjective description of a performance of *Withdrawal from Orchid Lagoon*. In "Jack Smith, or the End of Civilization" (published in the *Village Voice* of July 23, 1970), Mekas describes Smith's loft, the set, the uncertainty as to whether there would be a performance, Smith's recruitment of actors out of the audience and then his directing of them onstage:

> I suddenly was very conscious that it was 2 A.M. in New York, and very late, and most of the city was sleeping, even on Saturday night. . . . I began to get a feeling, it resembled more and more the final burial ceremonies, the final burial rites of the capitalist civilization . . . at 2 A.M., only Jack Smith was still alive, a madman, the high priest of the ironical burying grounds, administering the last services here alone and by himself, because really the seven or eight people who were now his audience (the other three were on the set) were really no audience at all.

Ultimately the actors leave in the middle of the piece. I was present at this particular performance. What seemed most memorable at the time was the piece's stunning conclusion. As the audience left The Plaster Foundation for the deserted streets outside, Smith turned up the volume of his record player so that one walked away with the sounds of the *Orchid Lagoon* theme, Les Baxter's "Quiet Village," slowly fading into the night.

Smith received somewhat more attention for his startling 1976 adaptation of Ibsen's *Ghosts*, which he transposed to "Atlantis" and called *The Secret of Rented Island*. In an interview published in the *Soho Weekly News* the week the production premiered, Smith asserted that "it is timely doing *Ghosts*. There are new strains of VD which will not respond to penicillin, you know. The play is a catalogue of wrecked lives, what people have done because they were afraid of what other people would say." He also revealed that, as of a few days before opening night, he had not yet fully cast the play. Indeed, *The Secret of Rented Island* may be the most radically pragmatic staging that Ibsen has ever received.

Regina was played by a large pink stuffed hippo suspended in a pulley-operated basket, Engstrand and Pastor Manders by a pair of toy monkeys, each seated in a little wagon. Mrs. Alving had a human interpreter, Ron Argelander, who sat, swathed in scarfs and a thick, black veil, inside a supermarket shopping cart. A prop-woman, made up as a hunchback, dressed in a kimono and wearing high, cumbersome wedgies, wheeled the animals and Mrs. Alving on- and offstage, positioned them (and also worked the lighting) as directed by Smith, who played Oswald.

Most of the dialogue was prerecorded on tape by Smith, using voices of different pitches that varied between a garbled hysteria and a ridiculously slow drone. Although the tape appeared to contain the entire play (with interpolations), it was not always audible, having to compete with the records of ocean sound effects and exotic music that were played simultaneously. Smith delivered his lines live, reading them from a tattered script. (Its pages eventually littered the stage, along with the handfuls of glitter he produced from a pouch inside his pants and dropped on the floor.) Although the inanimate actors were given different voices on the tape, Smith sometimes indicated who was speaking by, for example, shutting off a light when Engstrand spoke and turning it back on when Manders delivered his lines. I am told by someone who saw the production early in its run that originally there was no taped dialogue, but that all the lines were delivered by Smith through a hole in one of the back curtains.

Among Smith's alterations was the transformation of Oswald from a failed painter into an actor who cannot remember his lines. (Despite the fact that he held the script in his hands, Smith would repeatedly ask Mrs. Alving what part of the play they were up to.) Both reviewers who covered the event were struck by this extraordinary strategy. Gerald Rabkin, writing in the *Soho Weekly News,* pointed out that "*Ghosts* is not satirized or ridiculed: on the contrary. Smith seems to genuinely identify with Oswald's breakdown." Dan Isaac, who reviewed *The Secret of Rented Island* for the *Village Voice,* maintained it was

> the only theatrical occasion I have ever attended where I watched an actor do a self-destruct number on stage that meshed perfectly with his role, so that—in twisted contrast to Brecht's alienation effect—the

pathos that is unmistakably there belongs more to the performing actor than it does to the character he is allegedly creating.

I do not think that this was unconscious on Smith's part. When asked by Gerard Malanga in a 1967 interview who his greatest "superstar" was, he cited Mario Montez, who "immediately enlists the sympathy of the audience."

As with all of Smith's productions, *The Secret of Rented Island* appeared to be a cross between a rehearsal and a private ritual. Isaac reported that, at the performance he attended, Smith actively solicited the audience's aid in staging the piece, asking, "Am I under the blue spot now? Do I look blue?" and that later,

> somewhere after midnight, the other members of the company . . . tried to get him to wind it up so they could all go home. But he only glared at them and yelled into the wings: "If you have nothing to do—do it on stage!"

Most performances began with the burning of an enormous quantity of incense and ended, sometimes five intermissionless hours later after Smith had struggled through the entire script, with the playing of Doris Day's record of *(Once I Had A) Secret Love* and the parting of Mrs. Alving's veil to reveal a hideously grotesque mask.

The Secret of Rented Island seemed the fulfillment of two esthetic dictums found in one of Smith's early *Film Culture* essays: "The more rules broken the more enriched becomes the activity as it has had to expand to include what a human view of the activity won't allow it not to include." According to Smith, Maria Montez's films

> are romantic expressions. They came about because . . . an inflexible person committed to an obsession was given his way through some fortuitous circumstance. Results of this sort of thing TRANSCEND TECHNIQUE. Not barely, but resoundingly, meaningfully, with magnificence, with the vigor that one exposed human being always has.

Smith's *I Was a Mekas Collaborator* was performed for several weeks in the spring of 1978. In some respects it was the most self-referential piece he had ever staged. Dealing with the failure of art, with years of accumulated frustrations and grievances, it all but presupposed a familiarity with his biography: "Uncle Fishook" (Jonas Mekas), the "Mausoleum" (Anthology Film Archives), the "Pawnshop" (Filmmaker's Cooperative), and "the horror of rented island" (Smith's continuing vicissitudes with landlords) figured prominently.

Typically, the two performances I saw had elements in common but used them quite differently. On one night, Smith remained hidden from the audience, "broadcasting" a *Jungle Jack Radio Adventure*—that began "Calling all Nazis! Calling all Nazis!" and concerned the adventures of secret agent Sinbad Glick, sent to Rented Island on a special mission for President Roosevelt—as his veiled female partner performed a strenuously exotic dance through the Salvation Army living room that made up the set. At another performance (cited by Smith as "the worst I ever looked on a stage"), the dancer vanished early on in the proceedings, while Smith sat down in a wheelchair by an ancient radio console and listened to a cassette recording of himself reading from the text of *What Makes Sammy Run?* Then, working partly from a script, he taped a new installment of *Jungle Jack*. This soon began to merge with scenes from *Ghosts,* an enigmatic description of "the horror of Uncle Fishook's safe," and rhetorical asides on the problem of living in a condemned tenement. After randomly playing back parts of the tape, Smith wheeled himself to the rear of the stage, and the play apparently ended.

Both nights, Smith used the idea of radio in three ways: as a fantasy machine, as a generator of found material, and as an unfulfilled promise for two-way communication. In all three senses, the radio came to be his metaphor for art. The latter sense in fact is a recurring feature of Smith's work: Some performances of *Gas Stations of the Cross Religious Spectacular* featured a bearded man wearing a brassiere over his sweater who operated a "confessional" where members of the audience were encouraged to seek advice for their personal problems. Thus, in *I Was a Mekas Collaborator,* New York's listener-sponsored, call-in radio station, WBAI, was periodically parodied as Smith promised his "lucky listeners" a chance to respond later in the show with "phone-call gross-outs." However, on neither evening did this occur.

I Was a Mekas Collaborator lived up to its confessional title when Smith remarked several times during the second performance that "I think you will agree that the *Jungle Jack Radio Adventure* is a failure." One felt that he was not only speaking of his current performance, which courted disaster at every moment, but of his entire career. "No one ever talks about the problems of daily life and so daily life becomes exotic," he added, disclosing himself to be "Donald Flamingo, just a local personality trying to make a living." Similarly, "Inez the slave-girl"— a character in the *Jungle Jack Radio Adventure*, or perhaps the dancer who earlier performed—was revealed as "an office temporary."

The effect of the piece was at once funny and poignant, a testament to Smith's courageous unpredictability in deconstructing and expanding the rules of art. In an excerpt from *I Was a Mekas Collaborator*'s script, published as a manifesto in *Art-Rite* magazine, he advises us to

> let art continue to be entertaining, escapist, stunning, glamorous and NATURALISTIC—but let it also be loaded with information worked into the vapid plots of, for instance, movies. Each one would be more or less a complete exposition of one subject or another. Thus you would have Tony Curtis and Janet Leigh busily making yogurt; Humphrey Bogart struggling to introduce a basic civil law course into public schools; infants being given to the old in homes for the aged by Ginger Rogers; donut-shaped dwellings with sunlight pouring into central patios for all, designed by Gary Cooper; soft, clear, plastic bubble cars with hooks that attach to monorails built by Charlton Heston that pass over the Free Paradise of abandoned objects in the center of the city near where the community movie sets would also be; and where Maria Montez and Johnny Weismuller would labor to dissolve all national boundaries and release the prisoners of Uranus. But the stairway to socialism is blocked up by the Yvonne de Carlo Tabernacle Choir waving bloody palm branches and waiting to sing the "Hymn to the Sun" by Irving Berlin. This is the rented moment of EXOTIC LANDLORDISM OF PREHISTORIC CAPITALISM OF TABU.

Rehearsal for the Destruction of Atlantis

jack smith

Rehearsal for the Destruction of Atlantis, a Dream Weapon Ritual by Jack Smith, dedicated to Irving Rosenthal, was first presented at the Film-Makers' Cinematheque on November 7 and 8, 1965. The cast included:

THE LOBSTER   John Vaccaro

DANCER   Mario Montez

MEHBOUBEH   Jeanne Phillips

DANCER   Jack Smith

DANCER   Joel Markman

SIAMESE TWIN (1st nite)   Tally Brown

SIAMESE TWIN (1st nite)   Julie Garfield

SIAMESE TWIN (2nd nite)   Barbara Rubin

SIAMESE TWIN (2nd nite)   Babette Long

NARCO   Franklin Crowley

NARCO   Mark Safron

NARCO   Tosh Carillo

NARCO   Will Gay

Design: Tosh Carillo
Material for Vietnam Tape: David Gurin

Originally published in *Film Culture* 40 (spring 1966). Reprinted with permission.

TIME: *the present.*

PLACE: *Atlantis . . . a child's vegetable garden of foreign policy cadavers.*

The audience files in blindfolded. Their files are taken from them and the usherettes (very tough lesbians in matron uniforms) see that all blindfolds are in place. A man in the audience objects to his blindfold. He is roughly cuffed and manhandled by the usherettes into submission to the bandage. Chloroform could be used.

The house lights and music dim.

The curtains remain closed.

Over the PA a MAD VOICE:

"You are to imagine that you are a wino. This afternoon you were overcome by a fit of drowsiness and you slumped to the sidewalk. You lie there in the sun—baking and half asleep. Your skin feels oily. Your socks are clammy. Your head feels like a coconut—your eyes like sore rectums. You are uncomfortably hot but you lie entirely motionless. A police wino wagon drives up and suddenly, rudely, you are prodded by a nightstick. You are dragged to your feet. You had a bottle in your pocket that was deliberately smashed by the nightstick. All the way to the station you have to sit on a pocketful of broken glass with a wet pant leg. You are driven to a skyscraper prison. It is disguised to look like an ordinary skyscraper. As the wagon approaches it you perceive, beneath screens, bars at all the windows. The walls have widely spaced stripes of dark and light which make it look even more like a prison. Whether by accident or design or both.

"Inside your belongings are checked and you are ordered to get naked. Then you are herded through a foot-bath for athlete's foot. Then you are made to take a bath against your will and sprayed with DDT. Then you are kept in a cell for a couple of days—and then—after standing in line to be given back your possessions—you are released. On your way out you observe wino wagons passing to and fro in the streets—bringing other winos into the prison, all of which is no doubt to provide a flexible means of keeping the number of prisoners in the building at a constant level.

"This is your tiny wino role in the perfect operation of the threat under which we live. All because you have no ego, are overly sentimental about your mother—but thus the necessary punishment for having prisons is diffused among the population. O what kind of baboon sperm is exchanged among the populace that creates generations and generations of creatures chained to a bed. O creator! can monsters exist in the eyes of Him who alone knows how they were created—why they were created and how they might have avoided such a fate! That maintains a system that supports in impunity rats who complain of and turn in their fellows instead of working out one's problems oneself. The RAT, able to climb straight up, able to crawl anywhere, which *sneaks* its food, which has no control over its rectum—which lives in filth and has a receding chin—the true rat is one which (as well as informs) holds out on the others a slice of white bread (which to rats is like angel food cake) in the match tray beneath the burners of a stove while the others are dropping dead of rat poison—and runs away in panic if startled. And who, to support himself turns to the occupation of FEDERAL NARCO!"

(*Curtain slowly, silently opens to reveal the Siamese (North and South) twin queens of Atlantis [Vietnam.]*)

TWINS: (*In unison*) "Take off your blindfolds now. You are in Atlantis!"

(*One to the other*) "O let us smoke some of the marijuana that grows so abundantly and legally in the many extensive fields and plains here in Atlantis!" (*Other* TWIN *says:*) "O yes indeed it transports me to a magical paradise." (TWINS *call:*) "Mehboubeh, Mehboubeh—bring the pipe." (MEHBOUBEH *does. They establish that marijuana grows in both North and South Atlantis and establish which each one is. MEHBOUBEH leaves stage and they find they need a match—they ar-*

gue about who should go. They go get matches somewhere. MEHBOUBEH *returns. One strikes the match—it goes out. The other says:*) "You think you know how to strike a match. You think that simply by scraping a match across some sandpaper you can light a match. Well, you're wrong! What do *you* know of the centuries of science of progress, of the contributions of Madame Curie, Thomas Edison, Edouard Manet, Lewis Stone, or Edward Arnold. Of the Andrews Sisters or Maria Montez! Of Travis Banton or Van Nest Polglaze!" (MEHBOUBEH *goes on her knees trembling. U.S. federal* NARCOS *in rat masks lurk about in background in order artificially to surround the smoking of a benign herb with all the aura of illegality established with criminal evidence collected. For future purposes. . . .*)

(*A procession of* DANCERS *in white comes in—the lead* DANCER *carries a matchbook and chants:*) "As windmills upon the earth turn and turn again—so upon the sea sails fill and fulfill while the mysteries of the winds blow ever as they list. Rabbinical lore whispers betimes of wind angels that die as soon as born and it is said old hags still sell winds on knotted strings to superstitious sailors on wharves of Norway!" (*Match is struck and pipe lit. They puff happily—*MEHBOUBEH *enters with a tape recorder—she explains:*)

MEHBOUBEH: "Everybody in the U.S.A. wants to manufacture and buy tape recorders but no one wants to repair them."
TWIN: "But the manufacturers must be incredibly wealthy—what do they do with their money?"

(*Debut Detroit Style tape begins,* DANCERS *come onstage, and film is projected over them for a production number illustrating the tawdry waste of wealthy mfgrs. During the prod. no. the two* NARCOS *in rat masks are onstage spying.*)

TWINS: (*To* MEHBOUBEH) "What kind of moon is it tonight?"

(MEHBOUBEH *goes out—comes back—says:*) "The moon is full, Mistress." (*She goes back out and returns with the moon held as a platter and goes past* TWINS *to hang it up. As she passes them—they pick a paper off the moon—*National Enquirer*—headline: Mother Kills Twin So Other May Live.*

The next event:—the TWINS *become involved in a fantastic quarrel over who should get the arm of the armchair, which has only one arm. They end by dragging it clumsily offstage.*

The LOBSTER *enters with gigantic salad fork and spoon and crepe paper lettuce leaves. He arranges the lettuce leaves around the base of the throne platform, reciting a moon poem. Now the platform will be used as an operating table. After the moon poem the Vietnam tape commences to play.*

As Vietnam tape begins the TWINS *enter bickering, carrying pot pipe and newspaper. The rat* NARCOS *observe the pot pipe with magnifying glass and seize one of the* TWINS. *The other* TWIN *draws her space gun and covers her other half as the* TWIN *is dragged to operating table. They are severed with an electric circular saw. One dies right away. The other, the puppet, South-Atlantis lives a little while but expires in the* LOBSTER'S *arms, still holding the gun. During operation Mario Montez dances around operating table to music of Swan Lake.*

The LOBSTER, *in a daze, puts lettuce leaves over the bodies and tries to cover them. The* DANCERS, *smiling like chorus girls, come out one by one with the vegetables and place them on top of the littered operating table. The tape recorder and everything else in sight are piled in his arms and smoke erupts from top of platform as from a volcano, rises around the* LOBSTER *and obscures the stage, then the theatre, as the* LOBSTER *screams at audience:*)

"Put back your blindfolds—then don't—I don't care—get out I don't need you—Get out of my dressing room—OUT!!"

END

The Plays of Ronald Tavel

bonnie marranca

Ronald Tavel is somewhat unique among his off-off-Broadway contemporaries because he worked in films before he turned to the theatre. He wrote, and sometimes directed and acted in, numerous films
for Andy Warhol in the 1964–66 period. But Tavel is best known to most
audiences as a founder of The Play-House of the Ridiculous, which presented six of his plays from 1966 until its demise in 1967.

Tavel's more then twenty plays of the sixties and seventies divide generally into three categories: Film as theatre (early period), ex-
emplified by *The Life of Juanita Castro, Screen Test, Shower,* and *Kitchenette;* camp follies (middle period), which describes *The Life of Lady
Godiva, Gorilla Queen,* and *Arenas of Lutetia* (with some overlapping
with *Queen of Greece* and *The Ovens of Anita Orangejuice*); mythic or
symbolic dramas (late period), which includes *Boy on the Straight-
Back Chair, Bigfoot, The Last Days of British Honduras,* and *Gazelle Boy.*
Though Tavel's styles have divided themselves into these chronological patterns, many of the artistic and thematic concerns have remained
constant throughout his career.

Perhaps the most characteristic Tavellian device is his anarchic
use of language, which is sui generis in American drama. Tavel is a master punster and spinner of the multiple entendre (in *Gorilla Queen* and

---

Originally published in *Performing Arts Journal* 3, no. 1 (spring /summer 1978). Reprinted with
permission.

Arenas of Lutetia, especially); he also revels in sexual wordplay (most often generating homosexual imagery), spoonerisms, obscenities, literary conceit, distorted references to Shakespeare, allusions to grade-B movies, popular songs, and advertising slogans. A highly self-conscious dramatist, he devises a glorious alchemy of words to undercut all literary, political, psychological, cultural, and sexual categories.

In Tavel's dramatic world "play's the thing." Theatre is shown as theatre-in-the-making in virtually every one of his plays; the director even appears onstage in his early pieces. In the camp genre especially, the plays require extravagant costumes and sets and a broad acting style to draw out the performance-oriented texts. Tavel's Ridiculous aesthetic—the best example of pop art in the theatre—is a highly visual one in which verbal allusions frequently accompany visual puns; camp must be seen rather than be heard. The actors are called upon to exhibit an exuberant, to say the least, flair for tacky glamour and schlock imagery culled from the icons and images of Western society and its entertainments. The Ridiculous reflects the modernist—particularly Dadaist—preoccupation with pop culture. It is consciously "bad" art raised to the level of an aesthetic category. (It's so bad it's good.) The Ridiculous is an exaggerated politics of consciousness whose narcissistic stance could only have been taken by artists who felt themselves manipulated by, yet at the same time outside and critical of, the American cultural mainstream.

Tavel has his characters quote literary allusions and dialogue from movies; they re-create familiar poses that parody classical drama, melodrama, burlesque, vaudeville, and musical comedy forms as well. He resurrects the past in order to create a dialogue with it. His is quotation art, drawn from the "high" and "low" forms of Western culture where both are equal in the Ridiculous. It is iconographic montage built on the inversion of romantic and heroic images which saturate Western culture—myth demythologized.

This layer upon layer of distorted mirrors, inverting images two and three times over, is characteristic of Tavel, whose dominant theme is identity. The plays move continuously toward structures of unmasking or stripping away (*Shower, Screen Test, The Life of Lady Godiva, Big-*

foot, *Gazelle Boy*), their characters fragmented, uncertain personalities in a world that has no temporal, spatial, or human logic. Tavel's theatre is anti-authoritarian, anti-intellectual, anti-family, anti-religion. It posits a utopian, pansexual society peopled by presocialized beings. The Ridiculous is a love–hate affair with women, exhibiting an infatuation with their seductive power, but it is artists making fun of what they are afraid of. When the Ridiculous as style or attitude began to move into television, rock music, and the world of fashion, it was able to do so in a more liberating way, and to deal with many more levels of irony and contradiction in relation to sex.

In Tavel's world sex roles are continually blurred as men play women and vice versa. Nothing is what it seems. The author has one of his characters in *Arenas of Lutetia* mouth his own philosophy: "in an age rowing rapidly toward annihilation, who is without irreverence is without honesty." Unlike the theatre of the absurd, in which dramatic metaphors embody a moral vision, Tavel's Ridiculous world is a valueless, anarchic place that refuses to take life more seriously than as imitation of art. It is metaphysical burlesque. Remarkably then, after his faithless mood in the camp follies period, Tavel turns to questions of faith, to a more mythic, metaphysical exploration of human thought and behavior in the later plays. His interests extend more to the realm of ritual, theology, anthropology, and philosophy (*Bigfoot, The Last Days of British Honduras, Gazelle Boy*) than previously, though the concept of identity remains a major theme.

• • •

Tavel's first four short plays, all of them filmed for Andy Warhol, are characterized by the filmic metaphor. Yet, on the whole, they are less about making film than exploring human behavior. In *The Life of Juanita Castro* tensions and hostilities are uncovered when the Director (John Vaccaro) tries to pose a few hot-tempered Latins for a family portrait. The fixed-camera aesthetic of Warhol is behind the play, but its theatrical power makes itself felt when the Director starts to work on keeping his ensemble together. "This play should never be rehearsed," read the stage directions, offering a strong clue to a play about staging a play.

In *Juanita Castro* the Director and Juanita are played by men, while Fidel, Che, and Raul are played by women. Tavel gets a lot of mileage out of sexual variations on his characters—lesbianism, incest, homosexuality, machismo—mocking cliché images of both men and women, all the more comic since these are historical and/or revolutionary figures. Fidel's long speech, which an actor is supposed to improvise around, is a garbled mixture of revolutionary jargon spoken in a half-baked pidgin Spanish dialect. "Los productos 'Goya' son los mejores," he proclaims.

Juanita Castro is essentially a director's play. The Director is the one who orchestrates the moods and tempi of the performance by prompting improvisations from the actors, and provoking them enough to make them react *for real* to his manipulation. He tells the actors what to say, how to say it, what stage business to do. (For example: to Fidel, he says, "Now, blow some smoke in Juanita's face. Juanita say, 'Estupido' and cough violently.") The "reality" of the performance is the psychodrama produced by the interactions of director-actor, actor-actor: the antagonisms, face-slappings, repeated lines, competitiveness among actors and actor-director, etc. It's what's between the lines that counts, eliciting the hilarious moments, the real dramatic tensions. Since Tavel's script doesn't provide the gestures, attitudes, tones—how the actors carry out the Director's orders—reading the play is an incomplete experience. *Juanita Castro* has no "literary" value; it is meant to be performed. Part of its aesthetic is the incorporation of the audience as voyeur, watching, as it were, behind the scenes while the play is being rehearsed. *Juanita Castro,* more than including rehearsal techniques in the performance of the play, is actually showing the rehearsal as the play. The hostilities and grievances as well as the joys of the company are presented *in extremis.*

Shower appeared with *Juanita Castro* as the first of the Ronald Tavel–John Vaccaro collaborations (soon to become officially The Play-House of the Ridiculous). *Juanita Castro* was written as a curtain-raiser for *Shower,* though formalistically it is the more interesting piece. *Shower* is a spoof on the spy genre, comic and playful like television's "Get Smart." Two shower stalls dominate the stage in this saga of X-35 and Terene, who seems to be looking for her "cherry." Of course, the whole spy story, with its sexual puns and innuendo, non sequiturs, non-sense, and purposely awful song lyrics, hardly makes any sense in the logical frame of things.

But this is no ordinary story. For starters, there is a corpse who comes back to life, a mute Dummy who delivers the last line of the play, mistaken identities, a love interest between a private eye (named Dick) and the agent Miss Termite. One of Tavel's most-used techniques, un-masking, helps structure the play: Terene, the Terrible Tart of Terra Cot-ta, is found to be Lulu La Goulu, the Lady from LaLuna, and X-35, who is never found out, is referred to as Mark Stark, Mark Stark Naked, Mark Antony Stark Naked. To further add to the multiple identities are the real names of the actors making this "film," intermittently announced by the characters. Tavel's creations are like lovable, eccentric cartoon characters whose exploits are larger than life. X-35 sometimes acts as a narrator of the action—the dialogue devised like that in comic book "bubbles" at dramatic moments—for the audience. "Terene and Mark Stark Naked embrace madly, unaware that they are both being watched—by eyes filled with DESIRE!!!!!" he announces. *Shower* is pure fun, and Tavel is now just beginning to show how he plays with lan-guage.

Tavel's next play, *Screen Test,* operates on the same theatrical premise as *Juanita Castro:* rehearsal as play, with the Director manip-ulating the actors. But this time there is a sexual theme that domi-nates. The setup is this: A director is giving a screen test to an actress. But there are two actresses onstage, one of whom is a transvestite. One is situated in the foreground, the other in the background. The Ac-tress in the background never speaks but does all the movement, while the Actress (transvestite) in the foreground speaks and does the movement, too. The Director gives directions for line readings, poses, profiles, emotional renderings, character types, and so on. The notion of the dramatic situation alone is devastating: an improvisational per-formance that carries performance to its limits, as a competition not only aesthetically, but sexually as well, with the audience the immedi-ate arbiter of style.

Like *Juanita Castro,* its values lie in the realm of performance; as a text, its impact is in its idea. The dramatic tension exists in the comparison of the "real" and the "facsimile"—the mirror image of the transvestite and the actual woman performing the same action. Here again the piece is defined by its improvisational nature, with the Director responsible for the play's emotional tone. Tavel's examination of the gestures of gender behavior, in addition to being highly theatrical, is a clever idea that suggests whole new ideas of questioning about sex, role-playing, and human behavior. That the transvestite role was played by the well-known underground star Mario Montez, himself a parody of forties film star Maria Montez, opens up even more possibilities of interpretation: what is a woman?

Dependent on the suggestive power of the performers and the strength of the Director, *Screen Test* offers a variety of theatrical experiences, emotionally and aesthetically. It can also contract or expand, depending on the chemistry of performers and audience. The sexual dialectic—a simultaneous gesturing of transvestite and actress—draws the audience into the idea of the play, which goes beyond emphasizing the lie, the artificiality of acting. It explores the mask behind the mask, as *real* personalities compete with each other in the contest of posturing. A sociocultural treatment of "performance," *Screen Test* is a radical theatre piece for its day.

Kitchenette uses the film metaphor—the actors talk to a Filmmaker, he talks to them, arranges props, etc.—and the interest in identity, as in the earlier plays. *Kitchenette* isn't so much a *play* as a pretext for a sexual theme. It is also a spoof of domestic drama seen through the prism of the absurd. It is, as Tavel has admitted, a work made under the influence of Ionesco.

Here the focus is on two couples: Jo and Mikie and Joe and Mikey—female and male and vice versa. Jo and Mikie are wife and husband, *or* mother and son. It is unclear which. Tavel is obviously hoping to make a comment on role-playing, particularly in the first part of the play when Mikie falls into a demasculinized, childlike state after a sensual spanking over Jo's knee. When Joe and Mikey enter the scene in the middle of the play, the sexual confusion is compounded with the couples changing partners in between bouts of fighting. The gestural

Bonnie Marranca

language of the play is strewn with sexual innuendo and wordplay, further emphasizing its sexual ambiguity. Small wonder that Jo says, "I can't figure out what my part in this movie is."

In fact, no one in the movie seems to know what he or she is doing. One funny sequence has Joe say, "Mikey, Mikey, I just flopped in love with you!" after jumping on top of him. But he replies with, "Hey, let me up, will you? I ain't Mikey, I'm Mikie!" No sooner has this sexual tryst been completed than what began as an innocent marshmallow roast turns into "matricide on a mattress," with Mikie garroting Joe with a prop. *Kitchenette* is less interesting than Tavel's previous work, but it shows for the first time his Freudianism and focus on dramatic character and narrative. It is also his final effort with film as theatre.

* * *

Tavel's earlier *Vinyl* had moved more into the realm of character study. Here is a one-act play whose action falls neatly into two parts: in the first part a young hood named Victor is seen as a violent, vulgar, antisocial bully engaging in sadomasochistic practices and homosexual rage; in part two Victor is cured by the Doctor who, in using TV to show him scenes of gang rape and murder, makes him lose his taste for violence.

Vinyl is a psychological melodrama that draws the Doctor and police figures as "types"—socializing forces who are Evil because they destroy the individuality of Victor. It is the same kind of manipulation of audience/reader choice—against the institution or society and for the free character—that characterized such thematically similar films as *A Clockwork Orange* and *One Flew over the Cuckoo's Nest*. The exaltation of violent, anti-social characters pitted against a constraining social system (the Rebel-without-a-Cause syndrome) is typical for the era.

A few years after this play Tavel expanded on the power/violence/sex theme in *Vinyl Visits an FM Station*, whose violent images and S & M regalia are even more explicit than in the shorter play. Seemingly set in an S & M clubhouse cum radio station in Southeast Asia, the play makes an attempt to link American imperialism to the violence theme, but ultimately is not very successful because it is thematically unresolved.

Tavel moves into a new style with *The Life of Lady Godiva*, his first play in the Ridiculous/camp follies style. Though certain concerns of the earlier works remain, namely, showing theatre as theatre, the question of identity, verbal machinations, and obsession with sexual themes, Tavel now moves more fully into a camp style that parodies classical and modern forms of art, draws upon American popular culture, and features characters from the historical and cultural past. In general, as he moves into a world of fantasy that comments on our real world, his work becomes more irreverent, visually flamboyant, comically and sexually uninhibited, and focused on social myths. Now the plays burst wide open with a cast of hysterical, extraordinary personages revealed in the most unusual guises. "We have passed beyond the absurd: our position is absolutely preposterous," wrote Tavel in a program note for the show.

In *The Life of Lady Godiva* he turns a tale of rape, mistaken identity, and religion into "the hysterical adventures of Coventry Convent." Mother Superviva (in drag) leads the festivities, and assisting her are the legendary Godiva (in Gibson Girl dress), Peeping Tom, Sister Kasha Veronicas, a sex-starved nun who is the resident cobbler, Superviva's sheriff son Thorold, and Leofric, a Warwickshire Lord in S & M garb. In the structure of the play, which parodies medieval and Elizabethan literary conventions and movie Westerns, Tavel manages to blend medieval lore with references to television, New York City's Mayor Wagner, the *New York Post*, the Rockettes, and Franz Liszt.

Lady Godiva refuses to take itself seriously, preferring instead to exist as a blasphemous, anti-historical bit of liberated fun. The characters can't keep from referring to their roles in a "performance." When a divertissement is introduced into the play, Tom tells the audience that it has nothing to do with the rest of the play, that "its purpose is to give the other actors time to change costumes." Sister Veronicas has a marvelous line that simultaneously mocks the inanities of TV commercials and refers to the rape scene, which she covers with a screen: "We'll ban this scene to take the worry out of being close." If Lady Godiva doesn't take her midnight ride, still a nuns' chorus urges her on with a Rockettes routine, and a chorus of angels (Superviva, Thorold, Veronicas, and Leofric) singing: "Godiva! Godiva! Godiva! / Naughty nudies on a horse." Besides Tavel's ubiquitous puns, wordplay (Mother Superviva: "Nudity is the quintessence of essence, though it is sickrilegious to say so."), and jokes to make you groan, there are smart comments too. "Pornography will be accepted. But nudity shall never be understood." "Voyeurism—oh, it's a sitting back and watching proposition. A watching of yourself." Tavel's outrageous aphorisms belie his insightful remarks on performance and the audience.

Gorilla Queen, Tavel's jungle fantasy musical, was his first play to be performed independently of The Play-House of the Ridiculous (it was presented at The Judson Poets' Theatre after the Tavel–Vaccaro split in 1967). Gorilla Queen embodies all the general characteristics of the Ridiculous aesthetic, including use of American "popular" culture, campy theatricalism, literary wordplay, sexual exhibition, and studied tackiness. Parodying both America's immediate culture past and the classical past, it is a glorious pastiche of theatrical forms and a camp classic. This technicolor musical extravaganza is peopled by Queen Kong, Karma Miranda, Clyde Batty, Sister Carries, Paulet Colbert, the Glitz Ionas (a tribe of gibbons), and several others who become embroiled in the most notorious encounters the other side of the absurd. The end result is literally a three-ring circus, with three groupings of characters singing and dancing in three big musical numbers, the Glitz Ionas swinging on vines above the heads of the audience, and the inner drama of Clyde's metamorphosis. If you can imagine a show jointly staged by Busby Berkeley, C. B. De Mille, and Jack Smith, this is it.

Any attempt to look for a "plot" among the simultaneity of events that comprise Gorilla Queen is itself ridiculous. Suffice to say that Clyde Batty shoots Queen Kong, who is transformed into Taharah White Woman, is raped by the Corpse of Kong, and emerges as Clyde-as-Kong to marry Taharah. This fantastical story is further complicated by the fact that Sister Carries and Taharahnugi White Woman are played in drag, Queen Kong appears as an effeminate man, and Clyde becomes half-ape. "The junkel abounds with strange sounds tonight. So many curious ejaculations." Clyde's comment alludes obliquely to the pansexuality of the characters while at the same time playfully ridiculing the romantic conventions of Hollywood's jungle movie genre. When Sister Carries marries Clyde-as-Kong and Taharah (in a final curtain resolution), she caps the play's sexual anarchy with the words: "I pronounce you man and wife, or man and man, or ape and man, or queen and woman, or queen and man, or queen and queen, or ape and ape and up and up. . . ." *Gorilla Queen* closes with an epithalamion parody, and a gibbon explains, "Art ain't never 'bout life, but life *is* only 'bout art." Devoted to the notion of play, it is a child's vision of pure fantasy and wish fulfillment, life imitating art.

For the images of his rich fantasy world Tavel draws upon American mass culture to find the myths, entertainments, language, and gestures he would subvert for his vision of the world, a grade-B movie comprised of all the conventions of Hollywood. "This forties flick routine" is the way Sister Carries describes Tavel's brand of kitsch. Tavel's technique is to play off the audience's knowledge of Hollywood convention by creating theatrical characters who allude to a stereotypical movie world while at the same time inverting the perspective of that world. He shows them in situations that parody filmic conventions of musical comedy, romance, burlesque, and melodrama. Simultaneously, because they are always alluding to their performance, or stopping the action, or commenting on how the production derives from movies, the characters draw attention to the conventions of theatre. Tavel is always aware he is putting on a show.

If the characters parody certain styles of acting, they are also seen in musical dance numbers (tap, soft shoe, rock, Latin, and Rockettes routines), all the while, mind you, singing sexually provocative lyrics to popular favorites such as "Bicycle Built for Two." Much of the dialogue is obscene, comprised largely of sexual innuendo and phallic jokes, double and triple entendres on sexual themes, as if Tavel had taken to heart the notion that "the Word was made flesh." The dialogue (spoken in dialects that include Brooklyn, Caribbean, Portuguese, and Chinese) is also replete with literary conceits and puns, perversions of familiar sayings and recognizable movie-script speech, in addition to occasional rhymed couplets and iambic pentameter. This is not "normal" conversational speech, but a kind of "quotable" speech that refers always to something other than itself. By the same token, the gestures of the characters allude to movie-style poses (from horror films, south-of-the-border musicals, romantic films, etc.) or quote other examples of romantic convention and pop cultural expression. In one instance, during "The Cockamanie" dance sequence, the stage directions indicate the dancers' attempt to capture "the poses and low-brow 'gracefulness' of bathroom and kitchen-can decals." These few minutes of "ready-made" humor sound like the influence of Andy Warhol, which is just another good reason to view *Gorilla Queen* as pop art in the theatre.

Tavel's insistence on quoting conventional posing as an acting style demands that his theatre be a highly visual one. Furthermore, his language and imagery work together in sexual interplay, one irony enforcing another. The Ridiculous aesthetic, grounded as it is in the external realities of theatre, needs a highly visual orientation to emphasize its fantasy nature and its sexual ambiguity, as much as the importance of the interplay between audience and actors. In this play Tavel has outdone himself. Its dazzling verbal gymnastics, creative use of popular iconography, highly theatrical nature, and exultation of the pleasure principle make *Gorilla Queen* Tavel's most accomplished work in the camp style.

Tavel's next full-length play, *Arenas of Lutetia,* falls into the same genre, yet it differs from other camp plays in its lack of innocence and preponderance of aggressive sexual expression. The play joins Actaeon, Sebastian (St.), William Tell, Admiral Byrd, Cleopatra, and Lutetia (a bitch goddess) in a Roman-style epic modeled on Hollywood extravaganzas. The Hairy Christians form the chorus for this romance of kitsch that draws its iconography from both classical and contemporary subjects.

What Tavel has attempted is a mythical treatment of his characteristic sexual and artistic themes by building his story around images of the martyr St. Sebastian—he is the author in the play—and the tale of Diana and Actaeon. *Arenas* is Tavel in a thoroughly Rabelaisian mood; the one-liners and puns fly like a surreal Marx Brothers routine trying to gross out an Elks Club convention. He has let his obsession with sexual punning and inverting the meaning of words completely take over the play. With its aestheticizing of violence, obsession with sex, and hysterical wordplay, *Arenas of Lutetia* shows a more indulgent and mannered Tavel. When the Hairy Christians sing, "O mad pun which might disclose / The madness of our lives," it seems almost a relief that life doesn't imitate art.

Boy on the Straight-Back Chair marks a significant change in Tavel's writing style and choice of subject matter. While it deals with violence and includes some Ridiculous elements, it is a complete departure from the comic hysteria and cinematic metaphors of the earliest pieces. Situated in the barren landscape of the Utah desert, *Boy* is a lean, lyrical drama, more realistic than Tavel's characteristic style but hardly an example of Realism. It has an abstract quality of the kind that frequently informs Sam Shepard's plays, but one crucial difference between the two is that Tavel, unlike Shepard, is not nostalgic in his treatment of the mythic West. *Boy* is a powerful indictment of the American way of life (and death) and remains one of Tavel's finest dramatic achievements.

Boy is taken from the actual case of Charles Schmid, a young killer of the mid-sixties who cold-bloodedly murdered young girls and buried them in the Arizona desert. Yet he stands for all the young killers who go on a spree: the couple in Terence Malick's *Badlands*, Charles Manson and his followers, Son of Sam. Like Schmid, Toby of Tavel's play is short, a mole painted on his face; he is a braggart, a charmer, a "hero" of sorts who kills for pleasure. He says at the start of the play, "I keep looking for the action."

All of the characters in *Boy* (with the exception of Toby) are seated in two semicircles of chairs, one curved downstage, the other curved upstage. Toby stands on a high chair above them and from this vantage point systematically murders four teenage girls who wander too close to his "territory": Mary is crushed with a rock, Maude and her sister Lynn are choked to death, and May is knifed. The townspeople ignore the murders, even when they are confronted with the bodies. As Toby is choking Maude to death, his friends talk about how boring their town is and two of the mothers discuss how to remove clothing stains. No one will give Toby the attention he craves; they refuse to become involved.

"Listen to me, look at me, turn around and look at me, won't you! Won't somebody?" His early pleas fall on deaf ears. Romeo, Toby's friend, and the only normative figure in the play, realizes what is happening and doesn't turn away from it but he can't make the others acknowledge evil. Their apathy is complete, sealed. The people who inhabit the Utah wasteland—a few schoolgirls, their mothers, Toby's mother, and two hoods—are bored, listless, and valueless. "Action" is what they all want. But their artificial, commercialized environment has anesthetized them, turned them into human beings unable to respond intellectually, emotionally, or spontaneously to their surroundings. Stella, who, along with the other mothers, functions as choral commentator on the action and themes of the play, describes the landscape in these terms:

> Ranch-type houses, green-sprayed concrete lawns, sprawling super-markets, fresh fish frozen and powdered, shiny chrome, home sweet home, yes Sir, this is the land of the big rock candy mountain, the land of powdered milk and honey, the promised land, get along little doggie, yippie aie eh!

The rhythmic flow and evocative imagery in Tavel's language is a joy. But more important, the language offers a vivid critique of the modernization of "our towns" across America simply in its iconography. Rock 'n' roll music and country ballads, which interrupt the play's action, emphasize its themes and keep the audience at a distance. One of Tavel's main dramatic points—that American life is a living death—is expanded upon by a singer: "In a land of no one dying / Not a living soul to boast." The lyrics are a gruesome inversion of Bob Dylan's famous lines: "He who is not busy being born, is busy dying."

Boy's dialogue incorporates familiar pop lyrics; its longer speeches often seem like the "riffs" of rock music (in this respect, one can compare the play to Shepard's later *The Tooth of Crime*). Bits of advertisements, clichés, literary conceits, and sexual innuendo color the regional speech of these characters. Though for the most part the language is crisp and rhythmical, a striking example of the re-creation of colloquial contemporary speech in American drama, Tavel sometimes overindulges himself with his characteristic puns and play on words, which seem imposed on the characters rather than their own natural expressions. Nevertheless, the performance quality of the speech is one of the play's chief assets, for this is in a way a play about performance and the witnessing of events. Toby, atop his chair as if it were a stage, is a real performer. He wears makeup, acts like a punk rocker, and stages murders, complete with props, for an audience. His final triumph comes at the play's close when he turns on his "electric" chair before the crowd. "Rest your eyes on me" are his last words. *Boy on the Straight-Back Chair* is an important contemporary play that mixes the iconography of an artificialized landscape with the language pollution of mass culture in an uncompromising comment on Americans and violence.

Bigfoot is quite a different type of play. It proves for certain that Tavel takes risks by not settling in one comfortable style, even if the results are not always successful. In *Bigfoot* he is in the realm of theology and philosophy, which is one reason the play seems more a philosophical debate than a dramatic whole. Tavel asks many questions about Existence, Being, Faith, and Salvation in his attempts to confront the mysteries of life in this most symbolic of his plays. Set alternately in a monastery and a forest, and featuring a metaphysical search for the Abominable Snowman, *Bigfoot* is a complicated quest play that draws upon Pirandello, Jacobean drama, the Book of Genesis, Darwin, and horror movies to create its visionary world.

As the play opens a young woman working the lights and an actor argue about the production before they casually step into a scene (a monastery classroom) as it materializes. What follows is a contemporary transposition of the story of Jacob and Esau, which builds on the "twin" theme (seen earlier in *Arenas of Lutetia*) by introducing Jack and Esau, Alpha and Omega, and finally, Tavel's own brother Harvey (as deus ex machina) at the end of the play. The dialogue is particularly dense; a heightened poetic, sometimes pseudo-biblical, language that is the language of philosophy and theology. So much of what Tavel is trying to express in the play is in the exchanges of the characters who argue different positions on the questions posed.

Tavel's journey into the heart of darkness is obviously a very personal one for him, which explains why the vision of *Bigfoot* is so uncompromising and its series of reflecting images difficult to penetrate. Though *Bigfoot* supports a complex and expansive vision, its meaning and power often seem caught in its own far-reaching web of allusions, Tavel's investigation into the myths of knowledge weighed down by excessive intellection.

Bigfoot offers scattered glimpses of the heroic side of Tavel that is seen again in subsequent plays such as *The Last Days of British Honduras* and *Gazelle Boy*, which move further into theology, ritual, cultural anthropology, and evolution theories. Though in these plays he attempts to organize larger existential themes, they remain more inconclusive symbolic drama.

In *The Ovens of Anita Orangejuice: A History of Modern Florida*, Tavel moves back into another realm of the Ridiculous. Combining camp, social satire, and documentary, the play addresses real and fictional events surrounding Anita Bryant and her attempts to fight the issues of gay rights. There are scenes showing Anita shooting an orange juice commercial (backed by a chorus of oranges), addressing a congregation with the passion of a Baptist preacher, opposing gays at a hearing on the Dade County Gay Rights Ordinance, spreading her "message" on a television talk show. Much of her time is spent in a telephone booth making mysterious phone calls. Anita will try anything to advance her crusade. In one scene, she attempts to influence Chief Justice Warren Bugger [sic] to bring the issue of gay teachers before the Supreme Court. To Senator John Prig, who is running for governor of California, she proposes a surefire way to gain votes: "gays are the only contemporary scapegoat . . . Cause who else could you point to? Say a word in public office anti-blacks or spics 'n you've committed political suicide." Anita knows how to approach American prejudice. All the arguments she uses are attached to the twin pillars of American thought: God and country.

The notion of scapegoat is an important hinge for Tavel's larger theme: that the persecution of gays is analogous to the Nazi extermination of Jews. In the author's view Miami is the Berlin of the seventies.

The Ovens of Anita Orangejuice ends with Dade County voters entering polling booths (a symbolic refunctioning of the ubiquitous telephone booth mentioned earlier) set up in a pyramidal structure that uncannily resembles ovens. A red glow and faint crackling serves as grotesque counterpoint to Anita's "victory" speech which closes the play. It is the most horrific image in all of Tavel's plays. One significant fact pertaining to the characterization of Anita is that for all the perniciousness of her worldview, she is made to seem a pitiful, hysterical, misguided patriot rather than a personification of Evil. Tavel even seems perversely infatuated with her power and image. She is a woman made ludicrous by the hyperbole of her religious faith. In her "Kill a Queer for Christ," which closes Act I, Tavel accents her redneck fervor, devout Baptist faith, and homophobia in a long preacher-like tirade that builds to a stunning if formidable end. For a play that is considerably tame linguistically, in comparison to Tavel's obsessive verbal pyrotechnics illustrated in other Ridiculous plays, this speech shows the author at his agile best, using the very hysterical language of the "enemy" to cancel itself through its own sheer extravagance.

The Ovens of Anita Orangejuice is rather a peculiar play for the Ridiculous because it attacks society full face rather than through the inversion of images or language, as is usually the case. This play shows Tavel straining to bring direct social comment—not commentary couched in a subtext, allegory, or historical past—into the Ridiculous. It shows the Ridiculous approaching real social satire. That is not an easy task; in fact, it has made Tavel lean close to didacticism. In one sense, this approach contradicts the notion of the Ridiculous because it deals seriously with serious issues. That is why *The Ovens of Anita Orangejuice* moves more toward the grotesque than any other Tavel play. It is believable. It doesn't have the sense of comic anarchy that commonly characterizes his Ridiculous work; it is slower-paced, more linear, more preachy as it attempts to confront the audience with ideological concepts. Here is Tavel's passion transformed into compassion. Does *The Ovens of Anita Orangejuice* suggest the limitations of the Ridiculous in the face of direct comment on contemporary political issues? It is more likely that Tavel is stretching himself to include real, not merely playful, social critique in a more specific, straightforward Ridiculous manner. *The Ovens of Anita Orangejuice* is gay political theatre in the form of popular entertainment.

● ● ●

In Ronald Tavel's many plays he has continually switched styles and moved into new conceptions of drama, thematically and structurally. Yet, what has remained constant is his virtuoso manipulation of language, knowledge of dramatic conventions and popular culture forms, and unwavering sense of America's mythic pretensions. He demonstrates that the Ridiculous is both style and philosophy.

The Life of Lady Godiva

ronald tavel

The Life of Lady Godiva was first performed on April 21, 1966, at the 17th Street Studio, New York. A Play-House of the Ridiculous production, it was directed by John Vaccaro. The cast included:

NUNS' CHORUS   Sister Flossie of the Cross, Heller Grace, Regina Hirsch, Mario Montez, Margit Winckler

MOTHER SUPERVIVA   John Vaccaro

LADY GODIVA   Dorothy Opalach

TOM   Charles Ludlam

KASHA VERONICAS   Elsene Sorrentino

THOROLD   Dashwood von Blocksburg

EARL LEOFRIC   Tom Shibona

Set: L. L. Powers
Costumes: Jack Smith
Lighting: Bill Walters

Curtain, dark stage. Silence. Then a strong spotlight illuminates a very long chaise longue somewhat left of center. A small end table about 2½ feet high near the chaise, with a bottle of soda pop, a glass, an ashtray, a pack of long cigarettes on it, a Tiffany lamp suspended from above. Unless otherwise specified, the decor and costumes should be in Art Nouveau style. MOTHER SUPERVIVA *is discovered sitting in the direct center of the chaise; she is sitting up very stiff and proper, severe.* SUPERVIVA *is played by a male actor.* SUPERVIVA *is dressed in an English fin de siècle type nun's habit, with brimming hood, white bib, and blue gown.*

SUPERVIVA: You will discover that from this point on, every line is better than the next.

(*A very long pause.* SUPERVIVA *extracts a cigarette from the pack on the table, lights it in a long cigarette holder, and stretches herself out full length on the chaise longue.*)

SUPERVIVA: Nudity is the quintessence of essence, though it is sickrilegious to say so. . . . (*Long pause.*) Nudity is the most natural prerogative of the innovational spirit.

(*The spotlight weakens on* SUPERVIVA *smoking luxuriantly and flicking ashes and at this point the overture starts. It should be Art Nouveau music; if original music is not available, the end of Liszt's "Les Preludes" should be used. A strong spot lights upstage center. A sheer curtain with peacock feather and tendril designs is hanging there, and through it we can see a wooden white horse. The horse's body is very long, more than twice the length it should be.* TOM *is seated far up near the horse's neck, while* LADY GODIVA *is planted on the horse's rump.* TOM *is dressed with cap and jacket like a taxi driver. He has a coin changer strapped around his waist and dangling over his crotch. There is a steering wheel coming up from the base of the horse's neck, a rearview mirror coming out from its head, and a brake coming up from its side; gas pedal also on the flank.* TOM *has both his hands on the steering wheel.* GODIVA, *a buxom beauty, is dressed in a Gibson Girl gown with lace collar coming up to her chin; Gibson Girl hairdo. Both sit for a tableau vivant until the overture finishes. Then they both speak with an exaggerated British accent.*)

GODIVA: (*Laughing*) Did you say *big?* Why, my dear, it was one of the pillars of civilization!!

TOM: And then what happened?

GODIVA: Then when?

TOM: When there was nothing else left to pull off?

GODIVA: Why, then we pulled off the curtains—and let the sunlight in!!

(*Both laugh. Long pause.* GODIVA *takes out her lipstick and begins to apply it.* TOM *adjusts the rearview mirror so that he can watch her.* GODIVA *applies the lipstick vulgarly.* TOM *stares harder into the mirror. At this point* TOM *speaks with a heavy Mexican accent and* GODIVA *speaks English or Spanish with a very thick Brooklyn accent.*)

(*Suggestively.*) Yo may yamo Rosita . . . (*Sexy pause.*) Deesay!—Rosita!—deesay!

TOM: (*Clumsy*) Rosita.

GODIVA: Bu-ay-no! . . . Rosita Schwartzberger. Deesay!

TOM: Rosita Hamberger.

GODIVA: No! no! Schwartzberger! Schwartzberger! Rosita Schwartzberger. Deesay! Deesay!

TOM: Rosita Shortsbugger.

GODIVA: Correcto! Como say yamo?

TOM: Me Tom. Me Tom da cabbie.

GODIVA: Hi ya, Tom.

(GODIVA *continues to apply her lipstick.* TOM *stares madly into the mirror.* GODIVA *begins to lift the skirt of her gown slightly, exposing her*

Ronald Tavel

ankle. TOM *adjusts the mirror so that he can view her limb. He neglects his steering, seems nearly to crash head-on, swerves, they both get jolted.* GODIVA *recoups, resumes her suggestive lipstick application with one hand, continues to lift her hem with the other.*)

GODIVA: Soy professor day English . . .
TOM: (*Slowly, beginning to catch on*) Si?
GODIVA: Si. Key-air-ays kay tay day classes in English?
TOM: (*Slowly*) Si . . . como no?
GODIVA: Bu-ay-no. Yo resto a Hotel Hilton. Monyona por la monyana es bu-ay-no?
TOM: Si.
GODIVA: Moy bu-ay-no, Señor Tom Taxi-driver. (GODIVA *puts away her cosmetic, straightens her gown, and carefully gets off the horse's behind, carefully making the most, in doing so, of her own behind and other ample charms. Patting the horse's behind.*) That's what I call a real rump-seat honey. (*To* TOM.) Oh, Señor Taxi-driver, es ness-sess-serio a pagar?
TOM: A . . . a . . . no.
GODIVA: That's what I thought. Thanks, honey, see ya later. Sucker.

(TOM *remains seated on the horse and continues to steer. At this point the* NUNS' CHORUS *bursts into a choral background accompaniment.*)

CHORUS: (*Singing*) Guadalahooer! Guadalahooer!

(*The* CHORUS *keeps up this single-word accompaniment to the tune of* "Guadalajara." GODIVA *comes through the center of the curtains and sings the following song. If original music is not available she should sing to the tune of* "Darling, I Am Growing Old.")

GODIVA: (*Singing*)

Darling, I am growing thin!
I have lost my double chin.

I'm not what I might have been
Had I really learned to sin.

Darling, I feel kind of ill,
My physique is next to nil:
I seem short of verve and will—
Sex don't gimme no more thrill.

So rich knight and stately earl
Keep your diamond broach and pearl,
I'll no longer hump and swirl
—And that's why they call me the Gibson Girl!

(*The* CHORUS *dies out as* GODIVA *moves forward downstage.*)

GODIVA: Hello? Hello? Anybody here? You-whoo!! What a joint. Dead as
the morgue.

(SISTER KASHA VERONICAS *comes hobbling on from right, sweet old thing,
a bit out of breath. She is in English fin de siècle nun's habit, with a
cobbler's apron around her waist. She carries a candle.*)

VERONICAS: Coming, I'm coming. Just a moment, please.
GODIVA: (*Cheap*) Hi!
VERONICAS: Good day, my dear, what can I do for you?
GODIVA: (*Tough*) I don't know yet.
VERONICAS: (*Sweetly*) Well, my child, can I help you?
GODIVA: I don't know. Can you?
VERONICAS: I don't know. Won't you let me try?
GODIVA: Why don't you *try* on someone else! I'm looking for the Luz con-
vent.
VERONICAS: This is a loose convent. Won't you come in? (*They step
into* SUPERVIVA'*s spotlight.* VERONICAS *brings the candle close to* GO-
DIVA'*s face.*) Oh, my goodness, what are those bags under your
eyes?

GODIVA: They're my Saratoga trunks. I'm traveling light.

VERONICAS: Oh, I see. Now: how can I help you?

GODIVA: Well, for one thing, I need new soles on these oxfords. (*Taking off her shoes and handing them to* VERONICAS.)

VERONICAS: (*Looking down at* GODIVA's *bare feet*) Oh, I see you're going to want one-day service. Won't you please have a seat while you're waiting?

(VERONICAS *roughly shoves* SUPERVIVA *aside and she and* GODIVA *sit on the chaise to the right of* SUPERVIVA. VERONICAS *takes hammer and nails and new soles from her cobbler's apron and begins working on the shoes.* GODIVA *squats cheaply, like an uncomfortable whore. Both do not acknowledge the presence of* SUPERVIVA.)

SUPERVIVA: (*A little annoyed*) Mayor Wagner does it.

VERONICAS: (*Without looking up from her work*) How do you know?

SUPERVIVA: Because he had to get married again.

GODIVA: Boy, am I fagged!

VERONICAS: Been burning your bottom—I mean—your candle at both ends again, my child?

GODIVA: Well, I don't want to bore you with another wayside tale, but on my way here I stopped off for a minute and went into the bushes for an occasion, and it turned into an event.

SUPERVIVA: Some wayside tale: sounds more like a waylaid tail.

VERONICAS: Well, now, that wasn't so smart of you, was it, to go into the bushes all alone like that?

GODIVA: I know I ain't so smart. But brains aren't everything. A good pair of walking shoes can get you just as far in life.

VERONICAS: Of course, dear, and I'll have these oxfords soled for you in just two shakes of a bunny's tail.

GODIVA: I don't think I caught your name, honey.

VERONICAS: (*Cute*) Oh-ho: that's because it's not contagious.

SUPERVIVA: (*Sour*) Which is about all of her that's not.

VERONICAS: I am Sister Kasha Veronicas.

SUPERVIVA: The department of health, education, and welfare wishes to

The Life of Lady Godiva 43

acquaint you both with Lymphogranuloma Venereum. A venerable disease, to be sure.

GODIVA: Who's the old lady?

VERONICAS: Oh, that's Mother Superviva. She is the mother of all us sisters here at the convent.

GODIVA: I'm glad to meet a mother, anytime. My own died when she was struck by lightning, you know.

VERONICAS: (*Sweetly*) Well, if you have to go, it's nice to go quickly like that, isn't it?

SUPERVIVA: All persons with genital lesions should have a darkfield examination to rule out the possibility of mixed infections. Nothing is so necessary in blue-blood society as a pure contamination.

GODIVA: Bushes or no bushes, I'll skip the darkfield examination, if you don't mind.

SUPERVIVA: But it is best to be sure. If you can't be sure, at least you can be uncertain. It is best to be uncertain. Yes, I am certain.

VERONICAS: (*Very busy at the shoes*) Its main manifestation in tropical areas is yaws. What's yaws is mine.

SUPERVIVA: Sister Kasha Veronicas, don't you have the dishes to do? Remember—keep America clean!

VERONICAS: (*Flustered*) I have dishing to do, strictly clean, but Mother Superviva, I haven't completed cobbling these oxfords.

SUPERVIVA: How dare you talk back to me! I'd watch my step if I were you! I would remember the *Maine*, I would remember the Alamo and 44-69 or fight, if I were you!! Now, get off this set!

VERONICAS: (*Cowed*) Oh, forgive me, Mother, I am not wholly responsible for the sounds that issue from me.

SUPERVIVA: Issue those sounds in your private quarters!

GODIVA: Or from your private quarters.

SUPERVIVA: Sister Kasha Veronicas, begone!

(VERONICAS *hobbles upstage, muttering in bitterness for being scolded at, and goes through the sheer curtain. She seats herself under the horse's belly and continues to hammer away at the shoe repairing. During the following scene, something seems to go wrong with the mechanism of the horse and* TOM *has trouble with the brake and pedal. He dismounts and examines for the trouble in the horse's mouth, in its rear-end, and notably its pendant sex, which he cranks like a jack.* VERONICAS *works away unnoticing during all this, but when* TOM *is down beside her cranking, they take notice of each other, begin to get familiar.*

As soon as VERONICAS *leaves the chaise, a change comes over* GO-DIVA: *she throws herself at the feet of* SUPERVIVA *and pleads desperately. She will speak in her natural voice from this point on.*)

GODIVA: Please, please, Mother Superviva, I beg of you, let me take my final vows now!!

SUPERVIVA: (*Bending over, quickly*) First tell us who drugged Sister Kasha Veronicas!

GODIVA: (*Puzzled*) Who drugged Kasha Veronicas? Is she drugged?

SUPERVIVA: Hooer, you!

GODIVA: Who am I? I am Godiva. Lady Godiva.

SUPERVIVA: Lady, huh? Never knew the hooer who didn't claim she was a lady.

GODIVA: But I *am* a lady. I am Lady Godiva. Don't you believe me?

SUPERVIVA: Certainly not! I never believed that horse maneuver about Lady Godiva. So far as I'm concerned, it's all just a symbolic tale. Godiva divested herself symbolically: i.e., she stripped herself of her superfluous jewels in order to pay the levied tax.

GODIVA: You'll find my tail (*swishing her rump*) is not all that symbolic! Just wait and see.

SUPERVIVA: (*In a deep masculine voice, suddenly very lecherously masculine*) As a matter of fact, I am actually quite interested in pursuing my studies on the historical subject. (*Appraising her physically.*) I *do* have an open mind: I should be more than willing to draw new conclusions at the presentation of convincing facts.

GODIVA: You'll be able to draw and conclude in good time: only, please, I implore you, let me take my final vows now.

SUPERVIVA: What unambiguous temerity! How sickrilegious of a person of your profession to insist upon the vows! Where's your religious background, my child?

GODIVA: In the background, that's for sure. (*Singing.*) "And that's why they call me the Gibson Girl . . ."

VERONICAS: Kochel listing 2-4-69.

SUPERVIVA: Spare us the vocal specialties, canary, and just let me know what you've been doing to merit the veil.

GODIVA: (*Sadly*) These days I really can't say I've been doing anyone— I mean anything—except despairing.

SUPERVIVA: How nineteen fiftyish of you!

GODIVA: (*Wickedly, Brooklyn accent again*) Yeah, but you shoulda seen what I was doing in the nineteen fifties!

SUPERVIVA: Well, Madam Godiva, before I commit myself any further, you'll have to undergo a federal investigation. (*She blows out the candle on the table.*) Sister Kasha Veronicas!

(VERONICAS *is startled out of her intimacies with* TOM. *She breaks with frustration and adjusts her gown.*)

VERONICAS: Coming, Mother!

TOM: Coming down.

SUPERVIVA: Kindly desist from coming! Go and fetch me Thorold the Sheriff.

VERONICAS: For your—I mean—at your service, Mother. (*To* TOM.) You really don't have very many lines, do you, sweetie?

TOM: I guess I don't. You see, I'm still being groomed for stardom.

VERONICAS: Well, hang on, sweetie, I'm sure you'll make it.

TOM: Bye bye, bouncy.

(VERONICAS *goes out left.* TOM *sits twiddling his thumbs for a while and then resumes twiddling with the horse.*)

SUPERVIVA: Care for a drink, Lady, while we're waiting for the sheriff?

GODIVA: Well, I hardly ever implode.

SUPERVIVA: But are often imploded, I'll wager.

(GODIVA *and* SUPERVIVA *sit suggestively together on the chaise longue,*

and SUPERVIVA *pours a drink from the soda pop bottle into a glass.
She lights a cigarette and hands the glass to* GODIVA.)

Here's shit in your face, honey.

GODIVA: Thanks, Mother. (*She takes a small sip; an ambiguous expression awakens on her face.*) Er—what is it?

SUPERVIVA: It's celery tonic. Don't you like it?

GODIVA: Well, the taste is very Art Nouveau. (*She holds her nose and
drains off the glass.*)

SUPERVIVA: You certainly drank that quickly enough.

GODIVA: With some things, the sooner they're over, the better.

(SUPERVIVA *edges a little closer to* GODIVA. *She is dragging deliciously on
her cigarette.* GODIVA *squirms somewhat uneasily, confused by the
deep voice and masculine aggressiveness of* SUPERVIVA.)

There's a quarter in it for you if you can douse that cigarette without
burning me.

SUPERVIVA: What are you implying?

GODIVA: I'm implying nothing. Burn a hole in my new Gibson Girl dress
and I'll slap you with a fifty dollar bill.

SUPERVIVA: If you have one! (*Pulling away, now very defensive.*) Just so
there's no confusion, my dear, let me repeat: I am the woman of the
dunes. (*She clasps both hands on her falsies. Then she brings them
forward and places her bosom on the tabletop.*) And I rest my case!

(*A flourish.* VERONICAS *reenters downstage left with* THOROLD THE SHERIFF.
He is dressed in medieval sheriff garb.)

VERONICAS: Announcing Thorold, oldest sheriff in Warwickshire; His
Majesty's vice-squad viceroy to Coventry!

THOROLD: Chuck the fanfare, baby, I'm here on Fed business.

SUPERVIVA: (*Rushing up to* THOROLD *and kissing him*) Good Thorold, cast
thy nighted business color off and let thine eye look like a friend on
Coventry. Do not for ever with thy vailed lids seek for thy noble—

THOROLD: Chuck the fanfare, Mother, I'm representing the law now, and the law can have no friends, much less filial feelings. (*Feeling* SUPERVIVA *familiarly, of course.*)

SUPERVIVA: (*Enthralled*) My son, the Sheriff! So official!

THOROLD: (*To* GODIVA) Stand up, young lady!

GODIVA: (*Jumping up*) Young Lady Godiva, Sir!

THOROLD: No back talk. How do you expect me to investigate you with that Gibson gown on?

GODIVA: (*Humbly*) I bought it big sir, so it would be good for next year.

THOROLD: A chestful of frugality. Fill me in on your particulars.

GODIVA: They're hard to fill in, sir. I wanted to be a Playboy bunny. I wanted to be a bunny boys play with. A hundred times I filled out applications. (*Indicating her breasts.*) But the personnel department said there was nothing left for the imagination to fill out, and failed to hire me.

THOROLD: (*Coming on to her*) You have nothing to lose being a bunny . . . except tail.

GODIVA: (*Whorish again, Brooklyn accent*) I'm a two-time loser. So what's your pitch, copper?

SUPERVIVA: With two balls and no fouls you've got a strike. But tell her yourself, son.

VERONICAS: Yeah, Thor, tell the dearie.

TOM: Tell her, tell her good, Thorold!

VERONICAS: He must have improvised that line.

GODIVA: Well, Mr. Sheriff, I'm all ears.

THOROLD: I see you have a sense of English understatement.

SUPERVIVA: Thorold, I'd like to see you in my closet.

THOROLD: You've got the wrong play, Madam.

GODIVA: I said I'm waiting, Mr. Sheriff. What's the pitch?

THOROLD: (*Taking* GODIVA *around the shoulder*) Okay, baby, here's the pitch: and listen carefully cause I'm only gonna tell you once. Also, this is the exposition, so if you don't get it now, you're screwed, dig?

GODIVA: Shoot.

THOROLD: It seems this guy, Leofric (*pronounced Leff-ric*) Goodrich, has recently levied such a heavy tax on the local inhabitants that nobody can afford to patronize this establishment. You hip? Now, it's your job to charm this Leofric into remitting the tax so this business can get back on its back—I mean, on its feet.

GODIVA: What's in it for me?

THOROLD: You pull this off and you can take the veil.

GODIVA: I don't believe you.

THOROLD: Have you ever known me to lie, Lady Godiva?

GODIVA: No, never.

THOROLD: Well, there's always a first time.

SUPERVIVA: (*In heavy exotic accent*) Listen to him: he tells you the truth. He is not just standing around here waiting for a bus.

GODIVA: But how can you ask *me* to engage in such an enterprise? I am an artist. How can an artist forget about her art?

VERONICAS: Easy. Just put an "F" in front of it.

SUPERVIVA: (*Her conscience getting to her*) Pity we have to resort to these deceptions. Still, at any rate, it's a good thing hooers can't think and don't have feelings.

(*Suddenly a strong spotlight falls on upstage right. A grand flourish. We see* LEOFRIC GOODRICH *standing there, snarling.* LEOFRIC *is a bearded, tall, dark, and handsome leading man, dressed in sadomasochist leather outfit from head to toe. He carries a long whip, which he brandishes and cracks impressively. Everyone turns toward him.*)

VERONICAS: Announcing Leofric Goodrich, Earl of Mercia, Lord of Castle Coventry in Warwickshire, despoiler of the poor, divester of the tithes, and do-badder for Edward the Confessor, or so the latter hath confessed!

THOROLD: The very stud in question—go to it, Godiva!

VERONICAS: Good luck, Godiva girl!

SUPERVIVA: Con the convent's prosperity, my child; our future hangs upon your hips.

(*There is a chaotic scurrying for position:* SUPERVIVA *and* THOROLD *sit on the right end of the chaise and embrace rather Oedipally, mother and son.* VERONICAS *sits on the left end of the chaise. A space is left in the center where* LEOFRIC *and* GODIVA *will soon squeeze themselves in. Their lovemaking will constantly squash up against* VERONICAS *and threaten to throw her off the left edge.* TOM *mounts the horse in a single bound and steers madly.*

For the moment, LEOFRIC *comes rushing fiercely downstage and seizes* GODIVA *by the arm. He cracks his whip.*)

LEOFRIC: Ah-ha! my luscious, irresistibly lovely buxom box! You must be a lot of fun—with a little less fat.

GODIVA: Why do you grab me?—I won't run away.

LEOFRIC: When you find out what I am going to do to you, you will!

GODIVA: Je veux d'etre vedette [*Pronounced Je vedet vedet.*]

LEOFRIC: Never knew the hooer who didn't make some such claim. But a hooer is a hooer is a hooer is a hooer!

VERONICAS: Even if it *is* true, a gentleman doesn't say so.

LEOFRIC: Silence! No one has asked for your opinion.

VERONICAS: No one ever does.

LEOFRIC: What's your name, baby?

GODIVA: (*With heavy exotic accent*) Men, in their foolishness, gif me the name which means "beautiful."

LEOFRIC: In their foolishness??—in their blindness, you mean. Get on the couch!

(LEOFRIC *tosses* GODIVA *on the chaise and attempts to mount her.* VERONICAS *nearly gets thrown off.*)

VERONICAS: What the heck? And I got here early just to be assured of a good seat.

THOROLD: (*Hugging* SUPERVIVA) I'm glad we decided on the back row, aren't you, Mamma?

SUPERVIVA: Hmmmmm . . . sonny boy . . .

(GODIVA *struggles out from under* LEOFRIC, *desperately adjusting her collar and hairdo.*)

Ronald Tavel

GODIVA: Er, er—care for a drink?

LEOFRIC: If it's good and dry—or I'll stray lower where the real martinis lie.

GODIVA: That's a manhattan down below . . . (*winking at him*) if you catch my meaning . . .

VERONICAS: Some of the people you can fool all of the time.

SUPERVIVA: And some just when it suits the rhyme.

(GODIVA *pours a drink from the soda pop bottle and hands the glass to* LEOFRIC. VERONICAS *resumes cobbling the shoes.*)

GODIVA: Here's shit in your face, honey.

LEOFRIC: Thanks, hooer. (*He takes a small sip; an ambiguous expression awakens on his face*) Er—what is it?

GODIVA: It's celery tonic. Don't you like it?

LEOFRIC: Well, the taste is very Art Nouveau. (*He grabs his crotch and drains off the glass.*)

GODIVA: You certainly drank that quickly enough.

LEOFRIC: With some things, the sooner they're over, the better. And you better taste better than this!

GODIVA: What makes you think you're even in a position to judge?

VERONICAS: Position is everything in life.

LEOFRIC: Because I have good taste.

SUPERVIVA: So he claims. But scratch an American deep enough and you'll find a Philistine.

VERONICAS: Oh, I'll bet he has good taste and tastes good, too.

LEOFRIC: What's your line of business, baby?

GODIVA: I'm in the clothes line.

VERONICAS: A clothesline. How sweet. Yet dry. (*Hammering at the shoes.*) I'll have these hoofers soled in just the shake of two tails. Our repair policy: "Sex While You Wait."

GODIVA: Actually, Leofric, I'm a fashion model.

THOROLD: Seems to me Godiva would have more success as a calendar model.

(GODIVA *gets up and takes a model's stroll across the stage. Model mu-*

sic is heard in the background, counterpointed by the NUNS' CHORUS *singing softly, "Guadalahooer, Guadalahooer.")*

GODIVA: About this heat-wave time we start exhibiting our exciting new virginsfall creations. We're stressing virgin olive-oil wool fashions for great-great-grandmothers. The high price of the wares is intended to compensate for the limited market.

THOROLD: Imagine that: new fashion for virgin grandmothers by Lady Godiva of Coventry!

VERONICAS: (*Paranoid*) Wonder what he meant by that?

LEOFRIC: I'd like to see your wares for a hotter climate: like Bangkok— or Bumppussy.

(LEOFRIC *leaps up, seizes* GODIVA, *and hurls her back on the chaise.* VERONICAS *is shoved, by the action, to the floor.*)

Oh, Montana Mush! you're something I could really get my fingers lost in!

(LEOFRIC *falls to his knees and throws up the skirts of* GODIVA'S *dress. He kisses her bare feet savagely. She giggles.* TOM *giggles in unison. Then* LEOFRIC *pulls away suddenly and examines the bottoms of* GO-DIVA'S *feet.*)

Ever notice how much the sole is like the palm?

GODIVA: What are you doing—reading my future?

LEOFRIC: Yeah, I see a peace march in your future.

GODIVA: Wrong:—it'll be a ride.

(LEOFRIC *crawls up her legs, giving them a thorough investigation. But he loses his fierceness as he rises and waxes unexpectedly romantic.* VERONICAS *is sentimentally touched by proxy;* THOROLD *and* SU-PERVIVA *too involved to notice right now.*)

LEOFRIC: Ever have a lover before with a beard?

GODIVA: Yes.

LEOFRIC: Oh, you jade!—even that you've had.

GODIVA: Well . . . it's the neighborhood.

VERONICAS: (*Swooning*) Coventry's left bank!

GODIVA: I'd like to see you shave that beard, Leofric. I mean, so I can see what you really look like.

LEOFRIC: How ridiculous! Shall I shave that dog or that pussy or that bunny or that wooden horse's mane and tail so you can see what they really look like??!! This *is* what I really look like. *You* are not what you really look like.

GODIVA: I assure you, I ain't the bearded lady.

SUPERVIVA: Yeah, she ain't. But might be one or two here not so free from suspicion.

THOROLD: (*Giving* SUPERVIVA *a phial*) Here, have some Ban, Mother, it takes the worry out of being close.

(LEOFRIC's *hand has entered the exhausted* GODIVA's *bosom.*)

GODIVA: What *are* you doing?

LEOFRIC: Mean to tell me you don't know?

GODIVA: Have you ever read folk tales of Malaysia, Leofric?

LEOFRIC: Yes.

GODIVA: What?

LEOFRIC: (*Annoyed*) "Yam."

VERONICAS: How successfully she fends him off. It's very much like being in the Poconos.

SUPERVIVA: In the what?

THOROLD: Poke whose nose? I'm the law around here.

LEOFRIC: (*Hot and bothered*) Listen, give me an heir, or I'll give you the air!

GODIVA: That's just letting the fart from a loftier locale.

VERONICAS: That line was banned from an earlier version of this scene—to take the worry out of being close.

THOROLD: Hey, Godiva, you've worked his wanter up enough. You can spring the proposition now.

LEOFRIC: Who the hell are you?

THOROLD: I'm Thorold, Godiva's press agent.

SUPERVIVA: My son, the press agent!

LEOFRIC: Your son no less, and a press agent!

THOROLD: Make with the proposition, Godiva.

LEOFRIC: What proposition? What's this about a proposition?

SUPERVIVA: Go ahead, Godiva.

GODIVA: Listen, Leofric dear: are you really a virgin vampire? I mean, that is to say, do you really have a yen for that manhattan lying low?

LEOFRIC: (*Pulling away*) What of it?

VERONICAS: Oooooo—it's all so exciting!

GODIVA: Well, I didn't have the heart to tell you before, but you see, there's a string attached.

LEOFRIC: There's a lot of lace and bodice and crinoline and girdle and leggings too.—Okay, Miss Plumply Teasing, what's the string?

(*A noisy, melodramatic snatch of trumpetry from "Les Preludes" is heard.* LEOFRIC *stands up to his full fearsome height.* GODIVA *goes down on her knees before him.* SUPERVIVA, THOROLD, *and* VERONICAS *go down on their knees.* TOM *goes down on his knees, supplicating before the horse's pendant crank.* TOM *assumes the exact same kneeling position, angle, etc., as* GODIVA.)

GODIVA: O, beneficent Leofric, good and rich, Earl of Mercia and most merciful, movable Master of Castle Coventry and O worshipful Ward of Warwickshire, O remit the heavy duty that thou hast laid upon the peasantry in the hereabouts, that thereby relieved they might come hither to this house and further relieve themselves. Do thou this in remembrance of thine own lecheries. We four supplicate thee, then, for this.

THE FOUR: Amen!

TOM: Ah women!

(LEOFRIC *stands motionless for a moment, puzzled. Everything hangs*

*in suspension. He comes very slowly forward downstage. He paus-
es dramatically.—Then he undoes his garrison buckle, lets down his
trousers, adjusts his leather shirt, and zips up his fly again and fixes
his buckle.)*

THOROLD: Hey, Leofric, you wanna take that bit on tour?

SUPERVIVA: My son, the press agent!

LEOFRIC: (*The height of drama*) Ah, always and again there are strings
attached! Authority is postdated. Shall I reign forever in Mercia and
never be understood? Is it too much to ask that my every decree,
my every gesture be studied? How can you claim to serve me unless you comprehend the manner in which I pick up a pretzel after
taking a sip of celery tonic?

TOM: (*Poking his head through the sheer curtain*) James Dean is dead!

SUPERVIVA: (*Sadly*) Ah, well, one less mouth to feed.

(LEOFRIC *walks slowly back to* GODIVA *and lifts her to her feet.* TOM *rises
with the self-same motion.*)

LEOFRIC: What did you say your name was, my child?

GODIVA: Godiva.

LEOFRIC: Ah, Godiva. Lady Godiva. Then it is clear, my child, what you
must do. And my duty is clear too, the demand I must make is clear.
For all this was written in the mind of God and thereafter inscribed in
the history books long before either of us was born. And all these
things I re-rehearse in you that that which happens in the future may
be closer to you.

TOM: Oh, go on and tell her already.

LEOFRIC: Lady Godiva:—you must

THOROLD: Ride through the marketplace of Coventry

VERONICAS: At high noon

TOM: On the back of this old horse

SUPERVIVA: Stark naked!

LEOFRIC: And on that condition only can I remit the tax. You see, you were right, you were all right, you of this house against itself and me:—There are always strings attached.

VERONICAS: (*Very low*) Even if it is true, gentlemen playwrights don't say so . . .

(*A long pause. Everyone onstage maintains his position a little uneasily as if not knowing what to do next; as if there were really nothing to do next.*)

LEOFRIC: (*Unsure of himself*) Godiva, lay this rhyme to thy heart, by way of consolation: When the Queen rides from her den, so, too, ride all her men.

(*Another long pause. Everyone attendant upon* GODIVA'S *reply.*)

GODIVA: But, good Earl, how can I possibly ride through the marketplace of Coventry at high noon on the bare back of that old horse when I'm stark naked? I have hemorrhoids.

LEOFRIC: Do they hurt?

GODIVA: No; but they photograph dreadfully.

(LEOFRIC *removes a small tube from his left breast pocket and gives it to* GODIVA.)

LEOFRIC: Here, use this. In case of severe, prolonged irritation, consult your physician. In case of death, discontinue use.

(GODIVA *screams and faints to the floor.* SUPERVIVA, THOROLD, *and* VERONICAS *rise simultaneously as she falls.* THOROLD *rubs his hands with juicy anticipation.*)

THOROLD: The High Noon Nude Ride of Lady Godiva:—Ah! a press agent's dream!!

LEOFRIC: And now I must take my leave of this holy convent. I shall return when it is time to fulfill my half of the bargain. Adieu, O holy company.

(LEOFRIC *cracks his whip and disappears. The others breathe more easily once he is gone.*)

VERONICAS: Oh, my goodness, this whole thing has been so dramatic: I don't know if I can sustain the strain.

THOROLD: You've *sustained* more than this in your time, Veronicas, and you know it. This ain't nothin'.

SUPERVIVA: Yeah, it's nowhere. They got hotter shows every night at the Warwickshire Burlesque, and there ain't such a long buildup before they take it off, either.

(TOM *comes out through the curtain with a quizzical expression.*)

TOM: Is this the Coventry Convent Infirmary?

VERONICAS: (*Sweetly*) Yes, my good man, what can we do for you?

TOM: I have prickly heat.

(*They all laugh merrily and dance about in a gavotte.*)

I'm a Yankee Doodle Dandy, and Yankee Doodles often die. A real live nephew of my uncle lamb, scorned on the troth of your lie!

VERONICAS: You know, for a time there on the chaise, I mean when they were really going at it, Lucky Pierre had nothing *over* me. What was youse two doing?

SUPERVIVA: We was having Oedipus sex, sonny and me was.

VERONICAS: (*Firmly*) Dinner is served!!

SUPERVIVA: That's my exit cue!

THOROLD: Mine, too. I'm fagged.

(SUPERVIVA *and* THOROLD *rush each other out left.*)

VERONICAS: Tom, I'm starved. For affection, that is.

TOM: And all things thereto accruing. Sister, ya only gotta ask!

(TOM *and* VERONICAS *go out left arm in arm. For a second the stage is*

silent and dim over the prostrate GODIVA. *Then* TOM *returns immedi-*
ately and comes far downstage.)

Ladies and Gentlemen, this is the divertissement: it has nothing to
do with the rest of the play, but then, divertissements seldom do.
Actually, its purpose is to give the other actors time to change costumes. Basically, the divertissement is superficial—or superficially,
it's basic.

(TOM *clowns about briefly, his movements and manners very remind-*
ful of GODIVA's *walk, gestures, movements, and manners. Then he*
does a comic strip. His particulars remain undisclosed because he
never removes the coin-exchange which dangles down over them.
His efforts to remove his clothes without budging the coin-exchange
should be as excruciating as they are funny. Then TOM *goes upstage,*
permanently pulls aside one-half the sheer curtain, and mounts the
horse, not as a taxi driver this time, but rather imitating the tradi-
tional painting of Lady Godiva. He sits demurely and coyly on the
horse, unless otherwise specified, from this point on until almost the
end of the play.
    SUPERVIVA, THOROLD, VERONICAS, *and* LEOFRIC *reenter left, dressed as*
angels. They are carrying onstage an enormous ladder: this ladder
is wide enough to permit two persons to stand abreast on its rungs;
also, it has rungs on both feet. They huff, puff, and bicker, and final-
ly set the ladder up in the center of the stage. VERONICAS *has carried*
several stones onstage, which she places under GODIVA's *head.*)

VERONICAS: Take of the stones of this place, and put them for your pil-
lows, sweetie.

(GODIVA *rises momentarily out of her faint to adjust to the awkward*
stones.)

GODIVA: Oh,—er—much obliged.
VERONICAS: Forget it, sweetie, I get prop-man salary for that bit.

(GODIVA *falls promptly back into her faint. The others begin to mount the back foot of the ladder, one, two at a time. They caution each other to be very quiet during their ascensions, so as not to awaken* GODIVA. *When they reach the top of the ladder, they clumsily crawl over the top and begin descending the front foot. Then some go up and some go down, all with great difficulty, and, though they try to be serious and maintain angelic dignity, they constantly trip over each other's gowns, get in each other's way, etc., and make a generally messy show of things. When a certain picturesqueness of position has been achieved, they all freeze and suddenly burst into deafening song.* GODIVA *awakes with a frightened start and beholds the vision before her.*)

ANGELS: (*Singing*)

> Behold, we are with thee!
> With thee, evermore!
> Where e'er thou goest
> We're with thee most.
> Where now thou liest
> There thou shalt diest.
> Hear, what's our need:
> Spread thou thy seed.
>
> Behold, we are with thee!
> With thee, evermore!
> Innermost and nethermost
> We are thy host.
> We'll bring thee back,
> So now hit the sack.
> We don't wanna boast—
> But we're with thee most!!

(*The* NUNS' CHORUS *is heard singing in the background in counterpoint to the above song.*)

CHORUS: (*Singing*)

> Morning horniness!
> O, what corniness!
> That's the thorniness—
> When you awake,
> For goodness' sake—
> Morning horniness!
> Morning horniness!

(*The following repartee between the* ANGELS *and* GODIVA *should be a very rapid exchange up until the revelation.*)

GODIVA: What are you all—a band of Thespians?

VERONICAS: Lespians, did she say?

SUPERVIVA: No, my child, the males among us are saints, the females, saintesses.

GODIVA: Oh, I see.

THOROLD: Shut up: we'll do the talking. You see nothing! First of all, be advised that spontaneous outbursts of joy are banned in public:—the reason being that the Earl might pass through at any given moment and needlessly suffer his sensibilities offense.

SUPERVIVA: Pleasure is also against the law. All unauthorized pin-up girls found sitting on street curbs will be summarily picked up!

LEOFRIC: Your father was a rapist!

VERONICAS: Your ma a swinging sadist!

SUPERVIVA: What will be in 30 years? I look at you, Godiva, and I think, "What will be in 30 years?" I mean, if you don't get married soon and spawn brats, how shall it be with you in 30 years? You know what I mean, you know exactly what I mean—how shall it be with me in 30 years?

VERONICAS: We're selling subscriptions. Want to subscribe, Godiva? There's the Saturday evening post, there's the N.Y. daily post . . . most expensive is the entire weekend post, under the lamplight.

LEOFRIC: (*To* SUPERVIVA'S *come-on*) Please, Madam, one tittie at a time.

SUPERVIVA: (*Ignoring the snub*) You see, they used to think the bomb would solve everything. So everyone got lazy. But now they've forgotten how to make atomic bombs. All the taxes that used to go into military expenditures are currently being sunk into peace projects. So I repeat, what will be in 30 years?

LEOFRIC: Make up for lost time, but do not lose present time in the process!

(SUPERVIVA *lights up another cigarette after being snubbed by* LEOFRIC. *Her cigarette holder gets in* THOROLD'S *way.*)

THOROLD: Smoking again, Mother?

SUPERVIVA: Yes, Lord Raleighs. Ever notice he has balls instead of a beard?

THOROLD: Now listen carefully, Godiva: you are to be fairly forward with the angels, but within good taste, you understand? Sometimes you share a pleasantry with them, sometimes you pinch their cheeks.

LEOFRIC: You can dye your hair in the rear.

SUPERVIVA: 30 years hath September, April, June, and November. All the rest have 31 thousand millenniums, except February, which doesn't have any days at all—and, child, it never will!!!

THOROLD: I remember, I remember, Godiva, the house where we were born. And, believe me, I've done everything possible to forget it!

GODIVA: (*Despondent, confused*) I need a new nuance. Subtleties are okay in their place, but there's nothing like a nuance. A really new ance-er to everything.

SUPERVIVA: It is better to make use of everyday conceptions, and get double everything rolled into one.

VERONICAS: Some prefer cottontail candy.

LEOFRIC: And some a feminized dandy.

GODIVA: (*Impatient*) Listen, I ain't got all night! It's gonna be morning soon and I'll be waking up. Do or don't all you angels have some revelation to make?

SUPERVIVA: Yes, I do—I mean, we do. And hark me well, cause this is plot material. Good child, Godsend Godiva, sweet babe o'mine, I am your mother!

GODIVA: You are—?

SUPERVIVA: I repeat (*belching*) I am your mother.

GODIVA: My flesh and blood mother?

SUPERVIVA: Yes, my daughter, I am your flesh and blood mother. Rock-a-bye baby.

GODIVA: How am I to accept that?

SUPERVIVA: What's so hard to accept? Angelic revelations have contained much more shocking information—from time to time.

THOROLD: And I, therefore, good Godiva, am your brother. Your flesh and blood brother.

GODIVA: Well, that would follow logically.

LEOFRIC: Do not fret so, Godiva. Remember, an epiphany is just one god's opinion.

GODIVA: True. But that won't save me from the pickle this one puts me in. According to this play, Thorold is my brother. And Mother Superviva *is* my real mother. Waking or dreaming, there's no wiggling out of that.

SUPERVIVA: Ah, what a dutiful daughter! I knew she wouldn't deny her own mother. You see!

THOROLD: Or her mother and brother's request that she ride nude through Coventry. Or would she?

LEOFRIC: Well, Godiva, are you now willing to make your historic ride? Or do you have some legitimately defensible position from which to object to it?

GODIVA: It's hard to say where I want to divide the legitimately defensible position from my neurosis—although these days who could divide the two?

SUPERVIVA: My poor neurotic daughter! Hasn't your shrinker been of any help? Godivy, I do hope you're perfectly frank with your shrinker.

GODIVA: (*Shocked*) Really, mother—I try to keep our conversations on a high level at all times!

ANGELS: (*Singing*)

> Godiva! Godiva! Godiva!
> Naughty nudie on a horse,

Lovely limbed but slightly coarse,
There's no warrant for remorse—
We thy gallop strong endorse:
 So do what must be done
 And, doing so, have fun!

GODIVA: I will, but what is it that really must be done?
ANGELS: (*Singing*)

 Strip thyself of earthly dress:
 Topless gown we doubly bless:
 Angels at thy acquiesce
 Shalt thy nakedness caress!
  Then do what must be done
  And, doing so, have fun!

GODIVA: If God will be with me, and will keep me in this ride that I go, and will give me hair to hide, and raiment to put off, so that I come again to my mother's house a piece; then shall the Lord be my God: And this stone, which I have set for a pillar, shall be God's house: and of all that she my mother shall give me I will surely give the tenth unto Him.
VERONICAS: I take it she's gonna ride.
SUPERVIVA: Well, that's a weight off my chest!
ANGELS: (*Singing*)

 She'll ride! She'll ride!
 Hath thus decide
 For mother's hyde!
 So dignified
 A horse bestride,
 If Leofric's lied,
 Then matricide—
 Godiva tried—
 Is justified!

GODIVA: (*Singing*)

> I'll ride! I'll ride!
> Though tits collide
> And legs divide,
> I'm purified—
> Or mother chide.

ANGELS, GODIVA, and CHORUS: (*Singing*)

> Then naked, naked ride
> Thou daughter mother's bride!
> For naught remains to hide:
> Betrothal now abide.

THOROLD: Well, that's over with!

LEOFRIC: And the name of this city called Luz at the first, shall hereafter be called Death-el, Where She Rode, Arizona.

VERONICAS: Wonder how Tom's making out?

(LEOFRIC *comes up behind* SUPERVIVA *on the ladder and pushes her falsies practically up to her neck.*)

SUPERVIVA: Oh! I'm up to my chin in troubles!

(*One of* SUPERVIVA's *falsies falls out onto the floor.*)

GODIVA: You dropped a line, mother.

LEOFRIC: One could do worse than be a swinger of tits.

SUPERVIVA: (*To* LEOFRIC) Hey, could you change your rung?—you smell.

LEOFRIC: Sorry, madam, just having some fun, that foreign word.

SUPERVIVA: Well, go somewhere foreign and have it, if you don't mind.
    (*She pulls out the other falsie and casts it off, begins to descend the ladder toward* GODIVA.) I'm changing my channel, baby!

(*The* ANGELS *descend the ladder singing the last chorus, "Then naked, naked ride," over and again.* SUPERVIVA *advances menacingly toward* GODIVA, *divesting herself as she does, first of the angel's garb and, after that, of the nun's habit.* TOM *and* GODIVA *are both very frightened by this. Finally,* SUPERVIVA *stands revealed as a man. The others stop singing for a moment.*)

GODIVA: Why, Mother, are you making overtures?
SUPERVIVA: (*Deep masculine voice*) No, daughter, I'm going right into the first movement!

(THOROLD, VERONICAS, LEOFRIC, *and the* CHORUS *resume singing "Then naked, naked ride."* SUPERVIVA *seizes* GODIVA *and throws her to the floor.* TOM *falls to the floor by the horse in the self-same moment.* SUPERVIVA *falls on top of* GODIVA *and rapes her.* LEOFRIC *whips* VERONICAS *with his whip; she screams and rushes out left, still singing.* LEOFRIC *turns and whips* THOROLD.)

THOROLD: Shit! I wish this were a different play—like Shakespeare or something!
LEOFRIC: (*Whipping him*) Shakespeare?!—he belongs to the ages.
THOROLD: (*In pain*) Yeah—and this is one of them!

(TOM *writhes on the floor by the horse as if being ravished.* VERONICAS *reenters left carrying a dressing screen, which she places in front of the recumbent* SUPERVIVA *and* GODIVA *to hide them from the audience. But nothing hides* TOM's *ignominy.*)

VERONICAS: Enough of the sordid details. Some people have no modesty. We'll ban this scene to take the worry out of being close.
THOROLD: (*Ducking the whip*) Kindly desist, I beg of you, my noble Earl! I don't think you realize just how civil-minded I am!
LEOFRIC: Ha-ha! Don't you enjoy my kind of person?
THOROLD: Certainly—but you're the kind who's good in well-spaced doses!

LEOFRIC: (*Holding up contraceptives*) Sale on contraceptives! Contra-ceptives for sale! Soiled! Second-hand! Syphilitic! With holes punched in them!

(LEOFRIC *laughs demoniacally and tosses the contraceptives behind the dressing screen. Then he cracks his whip and whips* THOROLD *into lift-ing up the ladder and bearing it off stage-right.* LEOFRIC, *laughing evil-ly all the time, follows* THOROLD *out at right.* VERONICAS *is excited by all the goings-on and rushes about the stage irrationally.*)

VERONICAS: Mississippi dyke attacked by waves! Watch out for flying spumes! (*She spits at the audience.*)—Spumes as many as the vir-ginities that get lost at Niagara Falls!! (*She is pensive for a second, points to the screen.*) I'm supposed to cry throughout this whole scene . . . dreadful scene, dreadful scene!

(VERONICAS *checks out the writhing* TOM, *spins about, and slips out left. The singing of the* CHORUS *lowers dramatically and slowly fades out. A second of silence, and then* GODIVA *appears from behind the dress-ing screen. She is bedraggled, her dress completely twisted, her hairdo all undone. She is weeping.* TOM *rises, messy and worn, and remounts the horse.*)

GODIVA: Ah, all these years and this long life spent at nothing but an at-tempt to avoid that. That!—It was to avert just that, that congress, to sidetrack *her*, that I turned to prostitution! To love with all and thus love none, no single one; to love not—*with her!* And how has it prof-ited me?

(GODIVA *and* TOM *dry their tears.* VERONICAS *comes bouncing back in nun's habit, carrying a wig long enough to hang down to the floor.* GODIVA *does not turn to face her.*)

VERONICAS: But you do love all, Lady Godiva, you do wish to demonstrate your love for all. That is why you will take this nude ride.

GODIVA: Will I?

VERONICAS: Won't you? To save the people? I mean, isn't that what you want to do, Godiva?

GODIVA: That vision of angels got me so mixed up, I almost thought I knew what I wanted. But it is nice to have known once what you were doing, and to no longer now . . .

(GODIVA *submits stoically while* VERONICAS *adjusts the long yellow wig over her head. It flutes stiffly against her back.*)

VERONICAS: (*Very satisfied*) A perfect fit—and so stylish, too! So arty-farty!

GODIVA: Where'd you commondear this rug? Wigs—how I hate them! They make you look ten years younger, and feel ten older.

VERONICAS: (*Stepping out of character into the actress that she really is*) I am the rug-maker's daughter! Don't laugh—just think whose daughter you are!

GODIVA: (*Stepping out of character into the actress she really is*) For years the public has clamored to see more of me. This play answers their request!

(*At this point, the* NUNS' CHORUS *enters from behind the dressing screen, a chorus line of Rockettes of sorts. They are each wearing a floor-length wig over their nun's habits. The wigs so completely cover them, only a single eye of each is visible; this somewhat impedes their attempts at graceful movement.* GODIVA *turns toward them in surprise.*)

CHORUS: (*Brooklyn accents*) We hoid our cue.

GODIVA: What are they—male or female?

VERONICAS: If you can't tell, they ain't for you.

(*The striptease music starts and* GODIVA *and the* CHORUS *get in line ready to begin.* VERONICAS *stands aside watching.*)

TOM: Hum. Her mother must be real proud of her now.

(GODIVA *sings, and talks where indicated, this burlesque number, the* CHORUS *dances in the background.* GODIVA *strips slowly as she sings; when she has finished her number, she is nude except for the long yellow draping wig.*)

GODIVA: (*Singing*) Welcome to Boston!

> Shoppin' for the brand of boy
> Partial to the type of toy
> That Mama wants to give him on his birthday . . .
>
> I used to date those college guys
> That had their heads up in the skies,
> The kind that never used their eyes,
> Forgot to zipper up their flies:
>
> You gotta get your feet on earth—
> Come down off that upper berth,
> Believe me, College Joe, you'll find
> A lot of worth in this girl's girth!
>
> Hunters hanker after deer,
> Go great lengths and know no fear,
> But that healthy outdoor type
> Never shot my home-cooked tripe.
>
> Businessmen go ape for money,
> Got no time to suckle honey,
> Nothin's wrong with heaps of dough—
> Except there are other heaps, you know:

CHORUS: (*Singing*)

> Like that extra pound
> So long as it's around

That certain place
   —ain't ever outta place!

GODIVA: I mean, I used to wear these expensive off-the-shoulders type
   gowns: well, I been in a lot of parked cars in my day—and nobody
   ever nibbled on my shoulders!

Then there is the muscle man
Liftin' all the weights he can,
Workin' out in some hot gym—
Wastin' weights I've got for him.

Other fellas fancy poker,
Spend the night in smoky dens,
Leaving me at a loss to stoker
Up my fire with a poker.

What kind of a guy would I like to spend the evening with in front of my
   fireplace?—oh, any really manly type—like Rock Hudson, Rip Torn,
   Ed Fury, Chuck Steak, or Stark Naked.

Yeah, I'm shoppin' round and lookin'
For the fella likes home cookin',
For the boy who knows what's best:
Leg o'lamb, chicken breast.

Yeah, I've got a certain kind,
Special brand of boy in mind—
Just that homey type inclined,
Feelin' here and there, to find

CHORUS: (*Singing*)

That that extra pound
So long as it's around

> That certain place
>
> —ain't ever outta place!

GODIVA: And you better believe it:—I ain't the Singin' Nun!

TOM: Well, well. She acquitted herself professionally.

VERONICAS: Will you be getting any money for your ride, Lady Godiva?

GODIVA: (*Tough, resuming her Brooklyn accent at this point*) No:—I'm doing it for the exposure.

VERONICAS: (*As in an Elizabethan play*) Soft you now: here comes Thorold, the press agent.

(THOROLD *enters from the right; he is dressed as the Sheriff once again, but with a press agent's hat on.*)

THOROLD: Ah! Lady Godiva:—she keeps a tired businessman awake. Hey! how come you got so much hair?

GODIVA: I'm retentive.—Is that the nag I'm supposed to ride? (*Indicating the wooden horse.*)

THOROLD: Yes. Its name is "Vehicle." A vehicle well suited to your burlesque charms.

GODIVA: "Vehicle," huh? Is it male or female?

THOROLD: Kneel, my child, and know.

GODIVA: Skip the religious bit:—I had this convent pegged for what it is from the start.

THOROLD: Why, Godiva, how could you speak so lightly of this establishment? Why, this is holy Coventry Convent.

GODIVA: More likely Coventry Convention, and not so holy. Okay, okay, get the nag ready and let's get this show on the road.

THOROLD: Wait a minute, hold your horses:—I must announce you first. If you please, Madam.

(*Lights, a flourish, dramatic effects, the* CHORUS *quivering together.* VERONICAS *expectant,* GODIVA *very impatient.*)

Ladies and Gentleman! Presenting for the first time on any stage and

live before your startled eyes:—"The Life of Lady Godiva," a curtain-raiser . . . A difficult subject, handled with delicacy and taste. And relish.
TOM: Hubba, hubba!

(*A flourish, etc.,* GODIVA *moving whorishly toward the horse. Suddenly*
SUPERVIVA *reenters left on the arm of* LEOFRIC. *He is once again in his*
sadomasochist leather garb and is carrying his whip. SUPERVIVA *is all*
done up like the opera Delilah. She carries a huge pair of shears. She
and LEOFRIC *are laughing like well-heeled lovers. All movement stops*
and focuses on them. SUPERVIVA *flexes the shears.*)

LEOFRIC: And then what happened?
SUPERVIVA: (*Laughing*) Then when?
LEOFRIC: When you demanded of her that she go through with her his-
toric ride.

(SUPERVIVA *moves up to the* NUNS' CHORUS *as she speaks and begins cut-*
ting off their wigs, one by one, as if it were the most natural action in
the world. The CHORUS *line is too startled to defend itself adequate-*
ly. Her physical masculine power overcomes each objector and her
cries to desist.)

SUPERVIVA: Well, it was very much like Greek tragedy, you understand,
what with the audience knowing the whole story in advance and all,
and just sticking around to see *how* it would all come off, being all
along well advised, of course, of *what* was coming off. It's all in the
"how," not the "what." I.e., not the "what" am I, but the "how" am I,
the "how I live." But then, you see, with Lady Godiva of Coventry, one
of history's sexsational heroines, the Eternal Woman, etcetera,
etcetera, that need to have her personally love us, personally love
me, shall never really be fulfilled. Clip, clip. Ah, yes, it is an imaginary
perfection, however ardently sought, amongst our quotidian imper-
fections . . .

(*The* CHORUS *is scattered in outraged bewilderment. Their wigs, totally sheared, fall in heaps to the floor.* SUPERVIVA *surveys her work with satisfaction. Then she advances toward* GODIVA *with the awning shears extended menacingly.*)

GODIVA: (*Resuming her natural voice*) Who are you?

SUPERVIVA: I am Delilah—history's first female barber, and the Queen Bee of castration ladies.

GODIVA: I have submitted to you in everything. You turn your shears on me without provocation!

SUPERVIVA: Your cloaking, protective tresses are provocation enough, my child. Accept my apologies and kindly submit.

GODIVA: I do not like apologies. And I do not like the instances that necessitate them.

SUPERVIVA: Come, come, the morn shows the day, young harlot. You'll swim as well as Aquanetta soon as I've pared away your hindrances.

GODIVA: So—there are necrophiliacs in the tombs!

(GODIVA *steps back with unexpected quickness and wrests the whip out of* LEOFRIC'S *hand. She holds off* SUPERVIVA, *threateningly. The others all freeze where they are.*)

SUPERVIVA: Who *are* you?

GODIVA: I am she who has policed her own ambitions, Mother. I am the corpse you had in mind.

SUPERVIVA: What an active cadaver! Leofric—protect me!

LEOFRIC: I beg your pardon?

SUPERVIVA: I said protect me, defend me from that monster!

GODIVA: Of your filial making!

LEOFRIC: What did you say, Delilah?

SUPERVIVA: Don't you speak British, Earl Leofric, don't you understand me? (*Very frightened, rushing from one to the other.*) Thorold, you, my son, help me!!

THOROLD: What did you say, Delilah?

SUPERVIVA: Can't you comprehend me, either?

THOROLD: No, I can't. But I think you're repeating (*belching*) yourself.

SUPERVIVA: Sister Veronicas, Leofric—

LEOFRIC: Please, Superviva, words are an art form. Stop trying to use them to communicate with.

SUPERVIVA: (*Desperate*) Thorold! what should I do?

THOROLD: Look demure and coy, such is always effective when there are no appropriate stage directions.

VERONICAS: Or try snubbing everyone. That usually goes over in a pinch.

SUPERVIVA: (*Frantic, with* GODIVA *advancing on her*) Will nobody rescue me? I, who am the mother of all? Don't I get out of this tight spot?

LEOFRIC: I'm afraid you don't.

SUPERVIVA: That's funny: my friends never seem to read the same history books I do.

(GODIVA *cracks the whip and knocks the shears from out of* SUPERVIVA'*s hand.* SUPERVIVA *trembles in dread.*)

GODIVA: Your poetry is minor, Mother, your hang-ups major! All products to the test of market now!

SUPERVIVA: But, Godiva, think about tomorrow!

GODIVA: Why should I? Tomorrow never thought about me!

SUPERVIVA: You idiots, you ungrateful bastards, all of you! World War Three will teach you all a lesson . . .

(GODIVA *whips* SUPERVIVA *and pushes her down to the floor on her hands and knees. The others do not move.*)

GODIVA: In dreams the stopped blood of February has already begun mulling over the changing fashions of madness . . . Tally-ho!

(GODIVA *cracks the whip again and mounts* SUPERVIVA'*s back as if she were a horse.*)

SUPERVIVA: Godiva, think of what you're doing, think of the commitment you're making! You may have to live the rest of your life like this!

GODIVA: Mother, you may have to live the rest of your life.

The Life of Lady Godiva   73

SUPERVIVA: (*Crying*) Godiva, my child, my dearling daughter, have you no mercy for she who gave you birth? You are my flesh and blood daughter!

GODIVA: What do you mean your daughter? Have you ever seen me for the thing I was, stood to the side of the thing I am? What am I ever but a dream of you, fantasy versions of your own self, your projects down-decade projected and utterly minimized? I am fenced in the claustrophobic saddle of your back, like the whole wide world on the shell of a tortoise—you have never provided another place in your imagination for me to exist.

(*A flourish.* THOROLD *rushes up to* GODIVA *and gives her a riding stick.*)

THOROLD: Presenting Lady Godiva of Leicestershire, Warwickshire, Worchestershire, and Newark—New Jersey! Lady Godiva rides nude at high noon! Turn up the lights, will you? Full house lights on for high noon—let nothing, not a single detail be hidden!

(*The stage lights go up to their full brilliance.* GODIVA *stabs* SUPERVIVA's *side with the riding stick and begins to prod her into moving off as if she were a horse.*)

LEOFRIC: Godiva atop her named terrors, and by this act becomes she an adult.

(TOM, *with his special Peeping-Tom prongs and instruments, pries aside the sheer curtain and peers at the riding* GODIVA.)

TOM: (*In Mexican accent*) Hubba, hubba!

LEOFRIC: Who are you?

TOM: I am Tom, the Peeping Tom. *The* Peeping Tom of history, if you please. A voyeur, to you.

LEOFRIC: What does that mean?

TOM: (*Peering through a telescope*) Voyeurism?—Oh, it's a sitting back and watching proposition. A watching of yourself.

LEOFRIC: But you're playing the Peeping Tom on Lady Godiva.

TOM: So? If I'm watching her, she and I are the same person really. Ah! hubba, hubba! I mean, aren't we? I mean—that's me out there on the horse and I'm back here by the horse, not responsible at all, you see, but responsible of all, you see, an audience, a Godiva, of sorts.

VERONICAS: (*Cobbling the shoes*) He don't make horse sense.

THOROLD: Forget him, Leofric, he's just a brutish, imbecilic cabbie.

TOM: Hey, Leofric, how does this plot wind up, anyhow?

LEOFRIC: It winds up tragically. Despite her naked ride through Coventry at high noon, I never remit the tax.

THOROLD: You don't?—A bit of leather, aren't you, Earl Leofric? S-M at the fringes.

TOM: Bastard!

(*At this point, the end of "Les Preludes" begins to play. The NUNS' CHO-RUS reenters slowly from the left and slowly moves toward the right. There is something suggestive of riding movement in their steps. VERONICAS, frantically cobbling the soles of the shoes, at last completes her work. She rushes up to GODIVA and fits them on her bare feet.*)

VERONICAS: Lady Godiva, my martyred child, your oxfords are finally fixed. There, dear, that's it—so you won't be completely naked!

GODIVA: (*Sadly*) Thank you, Sister Veronicas. The only article I don't need, since I'm riding. Someday, have faith, Sister Veronicas, and pornography will be accepted. (*Smiling slightly.*) But nudity shall never be understood.

(*"Les Preludes" whelms up to a full blast.*)

GODIVA: Giddyup! Giddyup!

(*GODIVA rides SUPERVIVA out right with the NUNS' CHORUS following; TOM peeping with delight.*)

END

The Life of Lady Godiva   75

Theatre and the Ridiculous
A Conversation with Charles Ludlam

gautam dasgupta

Gautam Dasgupta: How would you define the term "Theatre of the Ridiculous"?

Charles Ludlam: It has to do with humor and unhinging the pretensions of serious art. It comes out of the dichotomy between academic and expressive art, and the idea of a theatre that revalues things. It takes what is considered worthless and transforms it into high art. The Ridiculous theatre was always a concept of high art that came out of an aesthetic which was so advanced it really couldn't be appreciated. It draws its authority from popular art, an art that doesn't need any justification beyond its power to provide pleasure. Sympathetic response is part of its audience.

    Basically for me, and for twentieth-century art, it's always been a problem of uncovering sources; it proceeds by discoveries. In my case it was based on a rigorous reevaluation of everything. Like yesterday, I was working on a sculpture, and Bill Vehr [an actor in Ludlam's company] stood over me and corrected me every time I did something that was in good taste. It's really an exercise to try to go beyond limitations and taste, which is a very aural, subjective, and not very profound con-

Originally published in *Performing Arts Journal* 3, no. 1 (spring /summer 1978). Reprinted with permission. Charles Ludlam died in 1987.

cept for art. And to admit the world in a way that hasn't been precensored. For instance, a handy definition for avant-garde art is that it's in beige-black-white-and-gray. Ridiculous theatre is in color; it's hedonistic. Different artists define it their own way, but basically it's alchemy, it's the transformation of what is in low esteem into the highest form of expression.

GD: Your early academic training in the theatre was rather traditional, wasn't it?

CL: I was a theatre major at Hofstra, and did the classics, staged and acted in them, and the rest.

GD: Was there a disillusionment with the naturalistic (or less expressive) theatre that led you to the Ridiculous style?

CL: Well, naturalistic theatre is a very recent innovation, a corrective device, and it wasn't the end of anything. It was a fashion to do things naturally. You can't really perform an unnatural act, unless you claim to have supernatural powers. So the whole idea of something being natural becomes a very oppressive concept; it's shallow. Gradually, through training with Stanislavski teachers, I realized that they wanted me to behave in a civilized manner in a room, and not do anything extraordinary. But everything I'm interested in is extraordinary.

GD: The technique of the Ridiculous is, of course, closer to expressionistic theatre or earlier modes of highly stylized theatre.

CL: Yes, and it seems now as if I wrote my way through history. I've written plays that were trying to revalue techniques from various periods. But ultimately, that is an academic approach, and modernism isn't about being academic; it is about being primitive. And becoming primitive isn't easy when you've been overeducated, overcivilized.
   Another fact is that all modernism was born in the theatre. Every

painting technique, everything we associate with modernism—for instance, Jackson Pollock's "scene-painting" techniques; and Salvador Dali's dreamscapes is like looking at a cyclorama, a barren landscape. Everything about naturalism is, in a sense, a distortion, because they (Zola, et al.) were reacting against the theatre of Sarah Bernhardt and others, and it made a mass movement. But finally it became too selective: it set out to prove a point, and proving a point is working from a preconception, and that is academic. Concept and execution is academic; going crazy and committing an atrocity is more modern. In the case of the Ridiculous, it is the only avant-garde movement that is not academic. It is not creating an academy out of former gestures and looks. If you look at today's avant-garde, it has an unmistakable look, and it moves more and more toward a vocabulary. It makes the art respectable, but it doesn't give us anywhere to go.

GD: But isn't it fair to say that within the Ridiculous movement your theatre seems to be more polished, less "mad" than, say, the works of Jack Smith, Jeff Weiss, and John Vaccaro? It is less anarchic.

CL: Well, in the Ridiculous theatre there was a highly competitive feeling among the practitioners, which did not encourage anybody new to do anything extraordinary. And in a way I'm very divorced from the work of the others. Since there's an element of almost demented competition among the various branches of the Ridiculous, which I think is way out of proportion and totally inappropriate, I had basically to go on and create the entire genre myself. As far as my work is concerned, I work in greater continuity—I've written, produced, directed, and acted in more works in the past ten years than the others. We were a group that continued to evolve in techniques, etc., and we built on our foundation. With the others there is the tendency to start everything from scratch, or else the individualism is so great, they can't work with anyone else. That attitude is good for research, the private attitude, but in terms of running a theatre it requires some sacrifice—not merely to exploit the moment, but to develop people, be loyal to them, and that's why our theatre got more polished.

Theatre and the Ridiculous   79

GD: Isn't there a danger of this stylistic refinement itself turning academic?

CL: Sure, but that is a question of the rigor one applies to oneself—you can do the same thing better and better, or do different things. The Japanese playwright Chikamatsu wrote on one theme, but just varied the context over and over and refined it. In my work, the panoramic quality saves it from academicism. It encompasses a much broader worldview, and I've been able to bring more material into my work. You see, there are different kinds of artists—innovators, masters, and journeymen—and some people are very good at uncovering little techniques, discovering fine points, while others, like myself, are able to organize vast amounts of material into a very solid body of work.

GD: Since you have drawn from the vast reservoir of dramatic and operatic literature, in both theme [*Hamlet* in *Stage Blood*, *Camille*, *Bluebeard*, and *Der Ring Gott Farblonjet* (Wagner's *Ring*)] and technique [Jacobean, epic, etc.], what makes these works of the Ridiculous different from, say, lampoon, parody, or satire?

CL: I think it's a question of depth and complexity. *Camille* could be taken as parody, but I perhaps have an ambiguous attitude toward these works in that while they are produced in a certain vein and in my own aesthetics, the thing to do is to examine the Ridiculous as if my work didn't exist, and then see what my work made of it. From my own point of view, there wouldn't be any Ridiculous if it weren't for me. There is a large extent of pain in my kind of Ridiculous. And there is a problem with pain. Aristotle defines ridiculous as the laugh of the ugly that does not give rise to pain. But pain has a lot to do with the significance of the work in our minds. How lightly does it go by? How easy is it to take? To what extent are you asked to suffer, the way you are asked to suffer in opera or a piano concerto? In my work there is both inner and outer direction. And the depth of involvement changes it from a mere spoof to something that transcends it. *Camille*, on the one hand, *is Camille*, it's a totally legitimate interpretation of the original, and I think the amount of personal anguish, how much of yourself are you going to reveal in it, is what makes it more powerful than just a spoof.

GD: Does this tension between the inner and the outer apply to the other actors of your company? Are roles handed out in the belief that such tensions will make themselves manifest?

CL: Yes. Another thing we are not talking about is that the theatre is a madly complex art form. It is not personal, and to make it personal one has to alter it or simplify it to some extent. Some people can control it, but it takes a lot of years. My early plays are more anarchic than any plays produced in this genre; my newer works are more classical. My early works had some classicism in them, but people couldn't perceive it then. It's not that they didn't understand the plays then, but that they didn't or couldn't see what went into creating them. And that's enough to drive anybody crazy: the distance between what you're experiencing while creating it and what the audience feels. Another thing is that today humor is in very low esteem. Today, the whole idea of humorous art is prostituted to such an extent that it can't be taken "seriously," that there can't be "serious humor." Now the whole idea of seriousness is awful to me—it sounds like something imposed from without. It doesn't really imply gravity or profundity; it implies decorum, behaving yourself, and that's what I don't like about it.

GD: So, essentially you're talking about an earthy, scatological, Rabelaisian sensibility.

CL: But what about the unbelievably sublime writing or acting that occurs? If you have shit in the play, and also have sublimity, you have a total panoramic view, like Dante (in his *Inferno*) or Shakespeare. Other artists want to slant the world one way. Now, I love belles lettres—Ronald Firbank, for instance, a sublime writer, so perfect in creating a small world—but other artists are bigger in a way, they encompass more, they encompass opposites. It's okay to say the plays are scatological, sure, but at the same time they do rise to heights of bliss and sublimity at moments for various reasons. You can't have highs without lows. The thing I'm against is appropriate and inappropriate material in art—it's shallow.

GD: Does it ever bother you to have to rummage through the repository of past art to come up with materials for your plays? This notion of cultural imperialism, of "quotation art." . . .

CL: Picasso said that no artist is a bastard. We all have forebears; we build on history, and rework it at times.

GD: But in the Ridiculous style there does seem to be an infantile regression at work, a pervasive and morbid sense of nostalgia for the movies of old, particularly Maria Montez movies. Could contemporary social and political events be dealt with in this genre?

CL: I don't see why art that has a history and a tradition is regressive. The danger is not so much regression; the danger is the morbid effect of repeating yourself, and that's where modernism—our contemporaries are Johnny-one-notes; each has a look (as in advertising) that he or she works for—comes in. Paintings begin to look alike in most galleries. They cater to people's need for the mass-produced, the reassurance you have when you go to a grocery store and you see a brand name. All of a painter's works today are supposed to look alike. This to me is insane tyranny; it is absolutely sterile, and that is more of a crisis to me than the problem of diversity, or what a friend of mine calls "virtuoso maximalism," the antidote that will supplant minimalism. Also, I don't want the savor of the art taken away, the actual enjoyment and appetite one has for creating something from something else, from something varied.

GD: Let's move back to the Montez films . . .

CL: With Maria Montez, as with pornography or anything held in low esteem, it's really a cultural prejudice; it's not inherently low. Those films were meant for children, and not that that's fine, but they were meant to be comedies and she gave her all. She gave the films a conviction, which was a fabulous quality to impose on something that most people wouldn't care for. The thing those movies have that today's movies don't have is actors sort of winking at you from behind their masks telling you they don't mean it. Not protecting themselves, not afraid to look foolish, not afraid to be thought mad. If actors then could seem to be possessed by their roles, they could justify any kind of theatrics, because the conviction of motivation was there to fill it out, this bigger form. Not everyone has that much life to fill a bigger form, and those who do become great performers. Now in naturalism there is always the tendency to be less than you are, to be more specific and less, and that was always a terrible danger. It certainly didn't work for me. I am able to do very lively, different roles.

GD: Your productions are indeed comic and lively, but some women find them deliberately caustic and painful in the way their gender is treated onstage.

CL: I think that's a misconception. I think women have traditionally been considered sacred, in a way, and that's something that had to go out the window if women were to become people. Women fare very well in my plays—they come out on top—but what people are disturbed by is female impersonation. They don't realize or understand its inner motive. They see something that is humorous; they don't understand what it means to play a woman. There's an incredible cultural taboo against it, particularly in Anglo-American culture. It takes a lot of courage to open yourself up to those feelings. Obviously, in a Ridiculous play everything is ridiculous, but the women in my company feel that they get a fair shake. And it's not so much as being against women as being skeptical of them and not taking a kind of blanket sentimental attitude toward them. Just the idea that women are equal to men doesn't mean anything; specific women have to be compared to specific men, and even then how can you compare two people? Even the idea of liberating women makes no sense to great women; it only appeals to women who have accepted rather conventional and erroneous ideas about their own existence because of economic factors and the like.

GD: Why is it that in New York most of the Ridiculous theatre has been created by homosexuals?

CL: Well, it isn't entirely male homosexuality though. Homosexuality is not a sexist phenomenon—so it's not homosexuals against women. And in the theatre there's always been a high percentage of homosexuals because, for one thing, to pursue a life in the theatre it's better not to have a family. Gay people have always found a refuge in the arts, and the Ridiculous theatre is notable for admitting it. The people in it—and it is a very sophisticated theatre, culturally—never dream of hiding anything about themselves that they feel is honest and true and the best part of themselves. NOTHING is concealed in the Ridiculous.
   Also, I think a company that was all-male or -female would immediately lower the level of artistic consciousness. It would turn into a social club, become political. Second, proselytizing lifestyles is a Brechtian thing—in the tradition of advertising and propaganda work—which doesn't have anything to do with the absolutely rigorous individualism that goes into our work. I think women are essential in Ridiculous theatre; if they weren't, it would be a partial view of the world.

GD: Why did you play the part of Camille and not give it to an actress in the company?

CL: I always wanted to play Camille. It had a lot to do with my feelings about love, and the nature of love in one of its highest expressions. Is love, in fact, self-sacrifice, or is there another way of expressing love? In my company we all encourage each other to do the roles we feel we must do. And sometimes people think it's sexism if you're in drag, but that's incredibly shallow.

GD: Do you think your plays could be performed by other groups without the overlay of the Ridiculous style?

CL: Sure, and they're done all the time, although I've never seen them.

GD: Of course, outside of the nature of the Ridiculous aesthetic, what makes your productions so overpowering is the emphasis placed on acting, the performer . . .

CL: Yes, that's exactly right. We always review the art of acting. Of the three branches that broke up—John [Vaccaro], Ronnie [Tavel], and I—John went and created a director's theatre, Ronnie a playwright's theatre in that he continues to write, and we created an actor's theatre, an acting troupe. In the long run, you can't get to the roots of conviction in a director's or playwright's point of view that you can get when the actors mean it. It takes years to develop that kind of understanding actors bring to your work, and that is what finally gives the work a base, a depth. Now of course each actor has his or her own style, but yet it's unified. Roles are constructed, they are not just arbitrarily given out, with careful planning as to what impression the role will create.

GD: Is the method of creation collaborative in nature?

CL: The script is up to me. I doubt if the process is unconventional, but a lot of groundwork is already taken for granted since we've been together so long. Also, unlike the avant-garde, I don't feel the need to have a body of theory to back up my work. I'm too much in the process of becoming something else all the time to do that. I'm constantly devouring things, so that no one approach ever quite becomes true for me for very long.

GD: Like the ventriloquist act [*The Ventriloquist's Wife*], another facet of the actor, the mask, another approach to the theatre . . .

CL: With Punch and Judy, and now with Walter Ego . . . I'm interested in the mask, what it can do—very objective. I was always interested in puppets, and then at one point it all came together and I knew I was going to turn ventriloquism to a higher and new purpose. It was a break-through for me, not the ventriloquism as such, but because it opened the door for something in the theatre that I had hit upon earlier in my work—why certain moments were more Ludlam, more my own. For one thing, it's opened up cinema for me. I had always kept a list of possible movie scenarios with my puppets, and I always saw cinema as a kind of puppetry.

GD: Does the name Walter Ego suggest the ultimate exposé—Ludlam and his alter ego on stage—that you think is a criterion for the Ridiculous theatre?

CL: Right, and also the fact that I recede a bit (the play belongs to Walter) gives me a nice perspective. See, the thing is you don't want to do the same thing forever, but you do. It's just little discoveries that keep you going. I really think of myself as an inventor who invents theatrical pieces. I don't think of myself as writing a play and then arranging a performance. I think my plays will probably become part of a standard repertoire because they were invented *in* the theatre.

GD: For a genre that is so stylized and expressive, your plays are a delight to read outside the context of performance.

CL: That's because they were born in the theatre. And also because of a sense of narrative. *The Ventriloquist's Wife* is, in a sense, pure theatricality. I was creating a piece for cabaret, and so I analyzed all that was the essence of cabaret entertainment, what made something work. I then realized that these things were essentially variety turns, and so I deliberately created a narrative out of them for maximum effect.

GD: To create a narrative is one thing, but to hang a Ridiculous-styled production on the scaffolding of some other earlier play becomes problematic. Say with *Camille*, your strict adherence to its narrative line makes one wonder if your treatment is deliberately parodic, or is it a new interpretation, or whatever.

CL: I don't think they are parodies actually. There is an *element* of parody, for parody is a way of reusing old things. But in order to do parody right, you have to do it as well as the original. That gives you the authority to make fun of it. Basically, I'm using these materials not to make fun of them, but because I think they are valuable.

GD: But is that serious intention clear in the mere fact of your choosing to do them?

CL: Well, the ambiguity of intention is probably just something in me. I don't know me or my work, and I don't want to know. It's revealed to me in flashes—the Dionysian element, if you will, whatever it is that creates it. It isn't a preconception; I don't set out to prove a theory. *Corn* came close to it, where I set out to make a point about eating food along the way, but the irrational, or better yet the intuitive element, must be the guide for me. You can't make a mistake with intuition. And as one matures artistically, one's instinct improves automatically. My plays are not parodic, but they *are* meant to be funny and humorous. There are perhaps subliminal effects that the plays have. I feel I do set up situations where the audience accepts A, B, and C, and then they are forced to accept D. It's gestalt, and, in a way, I change the culture by the way I force people to think their way through something. They went through the experience and they can't go back.

GD: Is it in that sense of subliminal change that Susan Sontag and Stefan Brecht have claimed that this sort of theatre is political?

CL: Yes, I think it is political, but what is political is perhaps misunderstood. Politics is about spheres of influence, and in that sense it is political. If a man plays Camille, for instance, you begin to think it's horrible, but in the end you are either moved or won over. You believe in the character beyond the gender of the actor, and no one who has experienced that can go back. In such cases, this theatre is political in the highest sense of influence. But as far as pushing for political upheaval goes, it's not true to the nature of art. Art is not meant to tear society down; it is meant to enhance it.

GD: Is that why you (and the Ridiculous movement in general) very rarely deal with contemporary social events?

CL: We have dealt with contemporary events, like the play on cryogenics, on euthanasia [*Hot Ice*] . . .

GD: But that's futuristic . . .

CL: Yeah, but *Camille* is a profoundly feminist work. Drag is something people today are prejudiced against, because women are considered inferior beings. A woman putting on pants, on the other hand, has moved up. So to defiantly do that and say women are worthwhile creatures, and that I'll put my whole soul and being into creating this woman and give her everything I have, including my emotions (and the most taboo thing is to experience feminine emotions), and to take myself seriously in the face of ridicule, that's it. That is the highest turn of the statement. It's different than wanting to make women more like men. It allows audiences to experience the universality of emotion, rather than believe that women are one species and men another, and what one feels the other never does. Even the women's movement is based on conflict and anger; my *Camille* is synthesis, an altogether different tactic. So you see, we do deal with contemporary phenomena. The historical thing is a pretext. The *Ring* has to do with power.

GD: Looked at in these terms, even the piece you did for the Paul Taylor Dance Company [*Aphrodisiamania*] seems to break down sex barriers. And also, based as it was on the Italian *commedia*, it seemed a logical direction for you as head of an "acting troupe" to move into.

CL: I've been doing a lot of research on Italian comedy over the years.

There are two ways of doing it. You can approach it as a sentimental thing, where you are trying to re-create a sense of what had gone on before, or you use those discoveries in a collision of techniques which create a new thing that means more to us. The thing about the *commedia* is that it is all resolved at the end—marriage is a happy ending, and no one feels that way now. That's one of the problems for modern comedy, to restore harmony at the end when so many values have been toppled down. So asymmetrical and irregular works have to be produced in order even to begin to evoke reality. But I'm more interested in the collisions of aesthetics.

A friend of mine said that the nineteenth century got it right—artists perfected art—while modernism is the history of getting it wrong. All the techniques of modernism—reduction, distortion, and so forth—are lending themselves to the inductive analysis of reality, of getting it wrong. When people describe a style of theatre, they are describing how it isn't like reality basically. They never talk about how it evokes reality, which is something we can't explain. I think my theatre is the most *real*, the most natural, but it isn't *realism*, it isn't *naturalism*. It's evoking reality by showing us what isn't real. If a man can put on makeup, false eyelashes and mascara, all the artifices of being woman, then obviously all those things are not part of being a woman. So something is created in that negative space, and that's where the mystery of reality is evoked. In naturalistic production, and even though I'm sophisticated enough to see what they're doing, I ask myself as an objective Martian looking at it: how much of it is intended? The moment they begin to use theatrical conventions, and there's no escaping that in theatre, I ask myself how much of it do they want me to take as real. Whereas in Noh theatre so much more is evoked, even to the extent of bringing convincing ghosts onstage. So that's part of theatre convention, when certain issues are settled and agreed upon, and only then can you get to more profound matters.

GD: At this point in the twentieth century, however, it seems that we've become totally immune to the collision of antithetical elements, parodies of conventions, shock, etc. How much more can we take?

CL: I'm talking about the notion of something perfected. See, once the idea of theatrical event and its convention is accepted for what it is and with relish, then everything is open to one. For example, certain women have tried to play Camille in modern times and failed because they were asking to be taken seriously. They were asking to be mistaken for the character in an everyday kind of way. So the audience thought they were being tricked. But if it's played in a manner that does not call for you to be a fool, that it's being created by, for, and of the theatre, then they are able to appreciate and accept a much broader amount of material. There is this theory in our century that any particular art form comes more and more into its own, as itself, its true nature. That paint is paint, paint is not a tree. The same is true of theatre, and the more the theatre comes to this self-realization of itself, the higher it becomes and the freer the subject matter. A political theatre can't do any topic because it hasn't come to terms with what theatre *is*. That's where the confusion arises—is it political or not, is it true or not? It doesn't interest me if it's true or not, it is just there. Even my ideas, I just try them on for size, to see if they work or not. Also, I don't care whether they're aesthetic or artistic because anything aesthetic or artistic is true only in so far as we've seen it before and have come to recognize it that way. But if we've never seen it that way before, it's only then that it gets to be interesting. When standards and values are no longer applicable.

GD: Wouldn't that be difficult to sustain in theatrical production?

CL: Yes, and one of my recent crises is that all my earlier works were based on an impossible conception to be fulfilled, and in the failure we found the aesthetic margin. How could it not be perfect? The end of that for me was Wagner's *Ring,* where I chose something impossible to do in one evening and succeeded. So now that aesthetic of failure cannot operate for me anymore. Whereas in the earlier *Turds in Hell,* the concept was to synthesize *Satyricon*—and three other plots to evoke actual demons and to stage a black mass—and it couldn't be done. The resulting mess and debris was the work of art.

I was always good at creating extremely original material by failing. Once you reach a point of succeeding, there is a danger because you realize you have become simply perfect, merely perfect. No progress anymore, and that's the frontier of consciousness. For me right now my works can no longer be destruct art, an art of failing. So then I realized I could go on expanding endlessly. My work pulsates that way—from expansiveness, epic-like, panorama to concentric, precise work. And now I'm on to a new phase. The adventure of creating a work in the aspect that has to be foremost—and that's the scary and the exciting part. The irrational and one's right to madness, that's the key. There has to be an element of danger, of risk, for the art to advance.

GD: You see theatre as therapeutic, don't you?

CL: It may be the illness . . . Ha! Ha!

Illustrations

Jack Smith in *The Secret of Rented Island,* a 1976–77 adaptation of
Ibsen's *Ghosts.* Photograph courtesy of the Plaster Foundation, Inc.,
and the Institute for Contemporary Art, P.S. 1 Museum.

Jack Smith in *The Secret of Rented Island*. Photograph courtesy of the
Plaster Foundation, Inc., and the Institute for Contemporary Art,
P.S. 1 Museum.

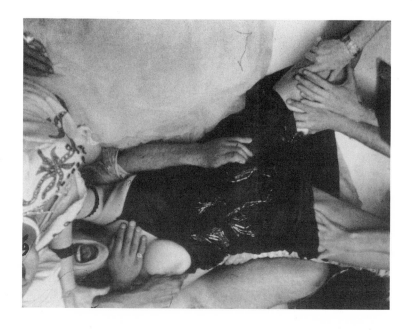

Film still from Jack Smith's avant-garde classic from 1963, *Flaming Creatures*. Photograph courtesy of the Plaster Foundation, Inc., and the Institute for Contemporary Art, P.S. 1 Museum.

Poster for *Shower* and *The Life
of Juanita Castro,* by Ronald
Tavel, early Play-House of the
Ridiculous productions,
directed by John Vaccaro at
the East Village's Coda Gallery,
1965. Graphic design by Jack
Smith; photograph courtesy of
John Vaccaro.

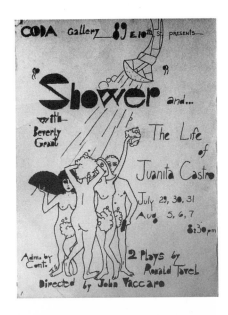

Scene from *Shower.*

Scene from *Indira Gandhi's Daring Device*, a play by Ronald Tavel, featuring a young Charles Ludlam, center. A Play-House of the Ridiculous production, directed by John Vaccaro. Photograph courtesy of John Vaccaro.

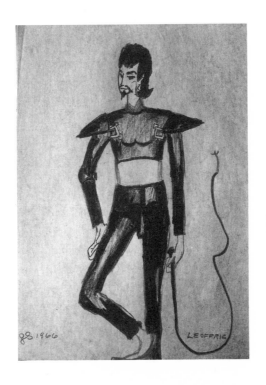

Jack Smith's costume design for the character Earl Leofric in Ronald
Tavel's *The Life of Lady Godiva*. Photograph courtesy
of John Vaccaro.

Charles Ludlam's *Conquest of the Universe,* a Play-House of the Ridiculous production, directed by John Vaccaro in 1967 at the Bouwerie Lane Theatre. Photograph courtesy of John Vaccaro.

Charles Ludlam and Lola Pashalinski in *Bluebeard,* which Ludlam
wrote and directed.

Scene from the Ridiculous Theatrical Company's celebrated production of *Camille*, with Ludlam in the title role.

Ludlam as Hamlet in *Stage Blood*. Photograph by John Stern.

Night Club by Kenneth Bernard, produced at La MaMa in 1970.

Kenneth Bernard's early play *The Moke-Eater,* directed by John Vaccaro in 1968 at the then-popular downtown club, Max's Kansas City.

The Sixty-Minute Queer Show, a late-1970s play by Kenneth Bernard, directed by John Vaccaro at La MaMa. Photograph courtesy of John Vaccaro.

Scene from Kenneth Bernard's *The Magic Show of Dr. Ma-Gico*, a Play-House of the Ridiculous production, directed by John Vaccaro. Photograph courtesy of Kenneth Bernard.

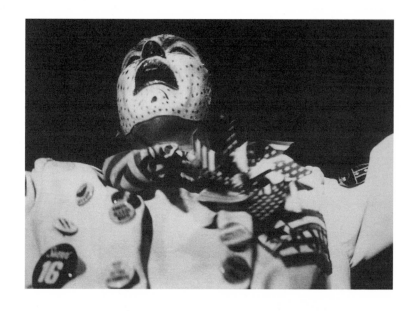

The Magic Show of Dr. Ma-Gico.

The Magic Show of Dr. Ma-Gico. Photograph courtesy of Kenneth Bernard.

Other "ridiculous"-style productions: *Heaven Grand in Amber Orbit* (1970), by Jackie Curtis, and *Cock-Strong* (1969), by Tom Murrin, La MaMa presentations directed by John Vaccaro. Photographs courtesy of John Vaccaro.

Stage Blood

charles ludlam

Stage Blood was first performed on November 11, 1974, at the Evergreen Theatre, New York. A Ridiculous Theatrical Company production, it was directed by Charles Ludlam. The cast included:

CARLTON STONE, an elderly player   Jack Mallory

CARLTON STONE, JR., an actor-manager, his son   Charles Ludlam

HELGA VAIN, a mature actress, Stone's wife   Lola Pashalinski

JENKINS, the stage manager   John D. Brockmeyer

EDMUND DUNDREARY, thespian   Bill Vehr

ELFIE FEY, a stage-struck, small-town girl   Black-Eyed Susan

GILBERT FEY, Elfie's father   Jack Mallory

GHOST   ??

Set: Bobjack Callejo
Costumes: Arthur Brady
Lighting: Richard Currie

ACT I: A Theatre in Mudville, U.S.A. Opening Day.
ACT II: Various Places Around the Theatre. The Following Day.
ACT III: Later That Night.

ACT I

*Scene: A theatre with the curtain closed. After the audience are in their
seats, the curtains part revealing a bare stage, riggings, and the glare
of a work light. Enter* CARLTON STONE, SR. *and* JR. *They are having a
heated argument.* STONE, SR. *is obviously drunk.*

CARL: Pop, please! Lay off that booze!

STONE: Don't nag me! You're worse than your mother.

CARL: We've got a show to do and you're no good half in the bag.

STONE: Son, I'm nervous.

CARL: You are nervous. What are you nervous about?

STONE: I'm nervous about being nervous. It's Mudville,* you know.
Tonight is Mudville.

CARL: Pop, you should be glad we're playing your hometown.

STONE: I didn't want to take this booking.

CARL: We needed the money . . .

STONE: I've got flopsweat! (*Drinks from a bottle.*)

CARL: Pop, put that stuff away! (*Grabs bottle and empties it.*)

STONE: (*Incensed, threatening with cane*) Are you crazy? That's good
liquor! . . . (CARL *returns bottle.*) I used to be Hamlet.

CARL: Pop, don't . . .

STONE: Now I'm just the ghost. Poetic justice. I'm a ghost of my former self.

CARL: Pop, you're making me feel guilty. I never wanted to play Hamlet.
It was your idea.

STONE: Someone had to play it. You don't want the Caucasian Theatrical Company to take its final bow, do you?

CARL: No, Pop, of course not.

---

*Or the name of the town in which *Stage Blood* is played.

STONE: What else would you do if you didn't act?

CARL: I don't know, Pop. I never thought about it.

HELGA: (*Off*) Where is it?

JENKINS: (*Off*) This way.

CARL: This is it.

(*A door at the back of the theatre opens and three somewhat weary and bedraggled theatre people enter, dragging some trunks with them down the aisle.*)

HELGA: There's something about an empty theatre.

EDMUND: Especially on opening night.

HELGA: Don't be sarcastic, Edmund. We were lucky to get a booking at all.

JENKINS: We'll be lucky to give a performance at all with no Ophelia.

CARL: Aargh, don't remind me!

JENKINS: Somebody's got to remind you. We need a new Ophelia by tonight and you've got to find one.

CARL: Don't look at me.

EDMUND: Jenkins is right, Carl. It's your responsibility.

CARL: But it was Pop's fault that she quit.

JENKINS: Yes, Carlton got us into this mess.

STONE: (*Quietly*) She was unprofessional.

JENKINS: (*Defensively*) She never missed a performance.

STONE: What do you call this?

JENKINS: Why, you old reprobate. You didn't understand her acting because she was Stanislavski trained. She works honestly and truthfully.

STONE: What do you know of honesty and truth? I call it lies and deception. Deceiving the audience into believing in surface reality, illusion. The great actor gives you a glimpse beneath the surface. Something that lies beyond your honesty and truth.

HELGA: Darlings, we don't need honesty and truth. We need an ingenue.

EDMUND: Maybe you should ask your Ouija board for the answer.

HELGA: (*Enigmatically*) Of course, Ouija never lies.

JENKINS: (*Exasperated*) Ouija! Ouija! Ouija! Karen is gone and all you can talk about is your goddamn Ouija board!

HELGA: In every theatrical company, there is always one damn fool who's in love.

EDMUND: (*Mockingly dramatic*) Ah, the agony. (*Calling.*) Karen! Karen!

JENKINS: That's enough.

(*All laugh.*)

(*Beside himself.*) I said that's enough! (*Turning on* STONE *with sinister intensity.*) I'll get even with you, Carlton Stone. If it's the last thing I do, I'll get even with you! (*Exits.*)

HELGA: Now now, Jenkins!

CARL: Leave him alone; he'll get over it.

EDMUND: I hope he doesn't go in the prop room and sulk for hours. The set's got to go up. We play tonight, you know.

STONE: Where are the dressing rooms?

CARL: I don't know. Let's find them. Take a break for lunch, everybody, and we'll have a dry run-through at one . . . if that's alright with you, Mother.

(HELGA *grunts in acknowledgment. All exit except* HELGA *and* EDMUND.)

HELGA: (*Looking up from her Ouija board*) "Something is rotten in the State of Denmark."

EDMUND: What's that?

HELGA: "Something is rotten in the State of Denmark." That's the line that's going to be flubbed tonight. Ouija says so.

EDMUND: (*Peeved*) But that's *my* line.

HELGA: And, according to Ouija, you're going to blow it tonight.

EDMUND: (*Helplessly*) Oh, for God's sake!

HELGA: Ouija never lies.

EDMUND: (*Pensively*) "Something is rotten in the State of Denmark." I've said that line hundreds of times and I've never gone up in it once.

HELGA: (*Darkly*) Well, you will tonight. Mark my words.

STONE: (*Reentering with* CARL) You may humbug the town as a trage- dian but comedy is a serious thing, my boy, so don't try that just yet.

CARL: But, Pop, couldn't you give me a few pointers? How do you play Hamlet?

STONE: (*Taking a recorder from his breast pocket*) Will you play upon this pipe?

CARL: But, Pop, I don't know how.

STONE: I pray you.

CARL: Believe me, I can't.

STONE: It's quite simple, you blow at this end, and cover the holes with your fingers and thumb.

CARL: I know that much. But I couldn't play a tune. The result would be mere cacophony.

STONE: Son, I can't tell you how to play Hamlet any more than I can tell you how to play this flute. In order to play Hamlet, you have to have *been* Hamlet.

Why, look you now, how unworthy a thing you make of Hamlet! You would play Hamlet; you would seem to know his stops. You would pluck the heart of his mystery. You would sound him from his lowest note to the top of his compass; and there is much music, excellent voice, in this little organ, yet you cannot make it speak. 'Sblood, do you think Hamlet is easier to be played on than a pipe? Call Hamlet what instrument you will, though you can fret over him, you cannot play him.

EDMUND: I'd like to do a murder mystery.

STONE: Why, *Hamlet's* the greatest murder mystery of all time.

EDMUND: What about *Oedipus Rex?*

CARL: Ah, yes, a great gimmick. The detective discovers his own guilt.

HELGA: The detective done it, huh?

EDMUND: Just like *The Mousetrap.*

JENKINS: (*Entering*) A man could make a fortune who could write a better *Mousetrap.*

STONE: But that's my point. *Hamlet* gave to the mystery story the one quality it had formerly lacked, the quality without which it could never attain greatness . . . a streak of the irrational.

HELGA: You mean the Ghost?

STONE: Exactly. Hamlet was not even sure that a crime had been committed, let alone who committed it.

HELGA: (*Enthralled*) A streak of the irrational!

EDMUND: Ah, yes, it seems today we had a streak of the irrational and it has left us without an Ophelia.

HELGA: Will the show go on?

STONE: Of course the show will go on. The show *must* go on! I will play Ophelia myself if necessary.

CARL: I don't know about that, Pop. We're doubling as it is!

HELGA: Why must the show go on? I've always wondered.

STONE: Actors must eat, and in my company, a day you don't act is a day you don't eat.

HELGA: I've never missed a performance. Be a darling, Jenkins, and hand me a sandwich, will you?

JENKINS: I'll see if the sandwiches have arrived. (*Exits.*)

STONE: Now you're talking about pot boilers, not Shakespeare.

EDMUND: Shakespeare wrote shameless pot boilers. That's why he called them *As You Like It, Much Ado About Nothing,* and *What You Will.*

STONE: Pshaw! Can you imagine a play entitled *As You Don't Like It?*

EDMUND: My point exactly. It wouldn't sell.

STONE: Are you denying the genius of Shakespeare?

EDMUND: No, I am only saying that in the theatre, genius is often wedded to a mountebank.

STONE: This is outrageous!

EDMUND: Come now, Carlton, great actor though you are, can you deny that you have ever stooped to monkeyshines?

STONE: How dare you! What you do to Shakespeare shouldn't happen to John Simon!

HELGA: Which brings us back to pot boilers.

EDMUND: And the irrational.

JENKINS: (*Entering*) And murder mysteries. Here are the sandwiches.

STONE: Faugh!

CARL: (*Grabbing the bag of sandwiches from* JENKINS) Well, what'll it be, Mother . . . ham or turkey?

HELGA: I'll take turkey.

CARL: I don't think turkey's good luck on opening night, Mother.

HELGA: Better give me ham.

CARL: You've got it. And don't eat the bread.

HELGA: Carl, I've only had two pieces of bread today—not more than eight hundred calories. . . .

CARL: (*Consulting a small notebook*) Mother, if my memory serves me, you have had exactly *twelve* hundred calories today.

HELGA: Impossible!

CARL: Salad dressing, Roquefort cheese . . . Goose-liver pâté! Admit the pâté.

HELGA: I admit the pâté.

CARL: (*Incredulous*) Banana Surprise!

HELGA: I wasn't surprised, I was appalled.

CARL: Mother, I'm afraid that if you eat those two slices of bread, you'll have gone over your limit. And you know what that means: no frozen skim milk later.

HELGA: Oh! (*Struggling with her conscience.*) Very well. No bread.

CARL: Oh, I'm proud of you, and because you were so disciplined, I'll see to it that you get strawberry.

GIRL: (*From the back of the house*) Excuse me, Mr. Stone, but I know the role of Ophelia.

CARL and STONE: You do?

GIRL: (*Still from the back of the house*) I know every line of it. I can do the "mad scene" for you, if you don't believe me. (*Entering down the aisle.*) "Where is the beauteous majesty of Denmark?"

(CARL *nudges* HELGA *with his elbow.*)

HELGA: Huh?

CARL: (*In a whisper*) Give her the cue.

HELGA: Oh, the cue . . . "How now, Ophelia!"

GIRL: (*Sings*)

> How should I your true-love know
> From another one?
> By his cockle hat and staff,
> And his sandle shoon.

HELGA: "Alas, sweet lady, what imports this song?"

GIRL: (*Going to* EDMUND) There's rosemary, that's for remembrance. Pray you, love, remember. And there is pansies, that's for thoughts.

EDMUND: A document in madness, thoughts and remembrance fitted.

GIRL: There's fennel for you, and columbines. There's rue for you, and here's some for me. We may call it herb of grace o' Sundays. O, you must wear your rue with a difference. There's a daisy. I would give you some violets, but they withered all when my father died. They say 'a made a good end. (*Sings.*) For bonny sweet Robin is all my joy.

EDMUND: Thought and affliction, passion, hell itself; she turns to favor and to prettiness.

GIRL: (*Sings*)

And will 'a not come again?
And will 'a not come again?
  No, no, he is dead;
  Go to thy deathbed! (*Points to* STONE)
He never will come again.
His beard was as white as snow,
All flaxen was his poll.
  He is gone, he is gone,
  And we cast away moan.
God 'a' mercy on his soul!

And of all Christian souls, I pray God. Good-bye you. (*Exits.*)

STONE: Follow her close; give her good watch, I pray you. (CARL *goes after* GIRL.) O, this is the poison of deep grief: it springs all from her father's death. (*Turning to* HELGA.) O Gertrude, Gertrude, when sorrows come, they come not single spies, but in battalions! First, her father slain; . . . next . . .

HELGA: Will somebody stuff this ham with cloves? This is our lunchbreak, and I don't want to rehearse. I want to enjoy my lunch in peace.

GIRL: (*Peeking out from the wings*) Well?

(*All stand dumbfounded for a moment and then* STONE *applauds.* CARL, who is behind the GIRL, *pushes her on to the stage. Everyone joins in the ovation.*)

STONE: Brava! Brava! My child, you can act! Can't she, Carl?
CARL: (*Nodding*) Yesiree.
EDMUND: (*Kneeling before the girl*) Please accept this rose.

(*It is a trick rose and it squirts the girl in the face.*)

STONE: (*To* EDMUND) You damn practical joker! (*To the* GIRL.) Your words came down on wings of inspiration, as if not learned by rote but like the very beating of your heart. (*Turning to* CARL *very excitedly.*) Carl, you must let her. You really must. She will play Ophelia! She must! Zounds! A talent like this comes along once in a lifetime. Oh, I'm out of breath. (*Gasping.*) Ah! Ah! Ah!
CARL: Jenkins! Don't just stand there. Get Pop's oxygen!
STONE: Ah, the excitement! Ah! Ah! (*He clasps the* GIRL's *hands.*) How fortunate, how very fortunate that you found us, that we found you. Oh! Ah! Ah! Ah! (*Gasping for breath.*)
JENKINS: Carlton, you're getting all excited. Calm down.
STONE: (*Icily*) You take a morbid interest in my health, Jenkins. I think you envy me my role.
JENKINS: You're paranoid.
STONE: Even paranoids have real enemies. I know you've been slowly tightening my armor.
JENKINS: You've been putting on weight, that's what it is.
STONE: (*Beating his forehead with his fist dramatically*) Aagh, what a curse it is to have the stage manager against you!
JENKINS: It's a good thing you don't have any food props or you'd think I was poisoning you.

(HELGA *starts and looks suspiciously at her hero sandwich.*)

STONE: (*Spitting dramatically*) "The funeral baked meats will coldly furnish forth the marriage tables."

HELGA: What do you mean by that?

STONE: If you want me, Carl, I will be in my dressing room. (*Exits grandly.*)

GIRL: May I play tonight, Mr. Stone? Oh, may I?

CARL: What's your name, sweetheart?

GIRL: Elfie Fey.

CARL: Not a bad stage name. What does your Ouija board say, Mother?

HELGA: (*At the Ouija board*) "Something is rotten in the State of Denmark."

EDMUND: (*Vaingloriously*) I won't go up in my lines tonight, I won't! (*Stalks out.*)

ELFIE: What do you think Mr. Stone? Do I have what it takes to be an actress?

CARL: Can you starve, Elfie? (*Turning to* JENKINS, *who has been muttering under his breath.*) What's the matter now, Jenkins?

JENKINS: When I talk, people won't listen to me.

CARL: If you would just . . .

JENKINS: Not get so emotional?

CARL: Try to talk a little more dispassionately.

JENKINS: I'm in charge. They gotta listen to me.

STONE: (*Reentering*) The other day you told me to shut up and when I did, you walked out of the room and didn't even say what you had to say.

JENKINS: If I said to you, "Carlton, shut the fuck up . . ."

EDMUND: They'd probably applaud. There's a conflict of power.

CARL: I don't think so. Pop doesn't want to be responsible for the stage management, would you?

STONE: (*To* JENKINS) Last night we were supposed to start at seven. But you didn't show up till seven. Everybody was ready to go.

EDMUND: Nobody thought we'd start at seven.

HELGA: I thought you said we'd start at eight-thirty.

CARL: It was never made clear whether we were supposed to be here at seven or begin at seven.

JENKINS: That should be made clear next time.

STONE: The reason I was late is that while on the telephone, I discovered that I had crabs.

HELGA: Echt!

CARL: I discovered my first crabs on the phone, too.

EDMUND: Like father, like son.

STONE: These were hardly my first! Twenty minutes before the dress rehearsal . . . I didn't want to infest my costumes because they wouldn't be cleaned for another week. Wearing those costumes every night, I knew I'd never get rid of them. So I went out and got some A-200 and all my makeup and went home and treated myself.

HELGA: Where did you get crabs?

STONE: Oh, Helga!

JENKINS: I think the show's in trouble.

CARL: But you thought the last show was in trouble.

JENKINS: Your old man should let me do my play. Can't you talk him into it?

CARL: All eighteen hundred pages of it? It would take weeks to perform. That plot isn't your tightest.

JENKINS: (*Showing a glimpse of an enormous script*) This is the tightest plot that has been constructed in the last four hundred years . . . No! . . . In the whole history of drama. Someday some poor sucker will be writing his doctoral thesis on the relationship between my writings and my bowel movements.

EDMUND: I had a psychiatrist who was very interested in my bowel movements.

STONE: (*To EDMUND*) That reminds me. You've got a dislocated diphthong. Instead of saying "I'm," you're saying "aum," or "om," or "ahm," or something. I find it jarring (*Sticks his fingers in EDMUND's mouth as he tries to say "I'm."*)

EDMUND: (*Almost strangling*) I'm. I'm. I'm (*Bites STONE's fingers.*)

STONE: (*Screams with pain*) Ouch!

EDMUND: I'll go over all my "I'ms" in the first act! (*Exits.*)

CARL: Pop, Jenkins wants you to do his play.

STONE: (*Heartily*) I would, if he'd cut it.

JENKINS: (*Pressing the script to his breast like a mother protecting her child*) Never!

STONE: In my boyhood days, I had enough of good reviews and empty houses. The story is everything.

Charles Ludlam

HELGA: That's what we owe our success to. Your father and I could always pick a story.

JENKINS: It would be a crime to cut this play. Besides, it's impossible. You can't cut one word. My plot is tightly woven like a hand-knit sweater: you cut one thread and the whole thing ravels. Why, this plot is tighter than Ibsen! Tighter than Scribe!

STONE: Tighter than a bull's ass in fly season?

JENKINS: Every new form seems formless at first . . . someday you'll see . . . Ah! What's the sense of talking to you!

STONE: (*Laughing heartily*) Talk! Talk! I'm listening.

JENKINS: What's the use?

ELFIE: What's the name of your play?

JENKINS: *Fossil Fuel.*

ELFIE: (*Venturing an opinion timidly but ever for the underdog*) I don't think anyone understands your work.

JENKINS: If they did, they'd hang me!

HELGA: (*Looking up from her Ouija board suspiciously*) What do you mean by that?

STONE: I am in the same predicament as almost all theatre managers throughout history. Actors of genius greatly outnumber playwrights of genius. Good actors abound; good playwrights are far to seek. The best actors of every generation have been forced to lean heavily on the classics and revivals of recent successes.

HELGA: A good melodrama!

JENKINS: Faugh!

STONE: But I prefer fustian, my boy, I do!

JENKINS: Mere bombast.

STONE: What's mere about bombast?

EDMUND: I always found Shakespeare too long and windy.

STONE: Yes, you wouldn't want to break your wind! (*Sits on a "farting cushion" which EDMUND has placed unbeknownst to the others.*) A pooh-pooh cushion! (*Throws it at EDMUND.*) You damn practical joker!

(*Everyone laughs uproariously.*)

HELGA: Tut tut! Falstaff farts in Shakespeare.

JENKINS: There were many playwrights in Shakespeare's own time—give or take a generation—who were far better than Shakespeare. Marlowe's mighty line, for instance, "And sooner shall the sun fall from its sphere, than Tamberlaine be slain or overcome." What of the forbidden love of John Webster's *Duchess of Malfi*, not to mention his invention of echo effects in the fifth act. Or Middleton and Rowley's *The Changeling!* Many scholars acknowledge these to be unique masterpieces, each one a distillation of an entire literary gift. These men wrote only a few plays. I have put everything into one!

EDMUND: In other words, it's your first play!

JENKINS: Well, I've got news for all of you.

ALL: !!!!!!!

JENKINS: The plays of Shakespeare were, in fact, never written by Shakespeare.

HELGA: Really?!

JENKINS: They were written by another playwright of the same name!

HELGA: Now that's a cue if I ever heard one.

CARL: That's my exit cue. (*Exits.*)

JENKINS: There's nothing as safe as Shakespeare if you do it straight.

EDMUND: But that's pure Bardolatry.

JENKINS: Bardolatry leads to Bardicide.

HELGA: Bard is box, darlings. It's as simple as that.

JENKINS: (*With disgust*) Box office! That's all you ever think of.

HELGA: Frankly, I think his box is bigger than his bite.

EDMUND: I'm for a good story with a message you can take home with you. And I'm sure that everyone in this company will back me up on it.

JENKINS: Of course, of course! Everyone will agree. But that's the M.D.R., baby, Minimum Daily Requirement: a good story that raises an issue. But what then, huh? Repeat the old forms? Never! (*Shouting like Lear.*) Recycle! Waste nothing! Do you hear what I'm saying? Cling to the Now through which all Future plunges to the Past!!!

(*Suddenly everyone is silent for a long moment.* JENKINS *becomes self-conscious.*)

EDMUND: (*Applauding*) Well played! Bravo, Jenkins! I say, quite a performance!

HELGA: Almost a Lear!

EDMUND: Yes, not quite a Lear.

JENKINS: You're all fools, fools! How long do you intend to go on hacking
it in Shakespeare? Dishing up culture with a capital K! How can you
go on pretending that there is a validity to monarchy, and that the
high-born speak sublime blank verse, while the poor and laboring
classes speak prose and doggerel?

EDMUND: (*Very bored and condescending*) Is that communism you're
espousing, Jenkins?

JENKINS: Oh, what's the use? Anything left of stage center would look
like communism to you!

EDMUND: I don't like politics. The theatre is like a religion to me.

JENKINS: Ah, yes. The art-religion . . . Out of the frying pan into the fire.

STONE: That *Hamlet* exists at all is a miracle!

JENKINS: It's a miracle we don't dissolve when we take a bath. (*To* STONE.)
This show's in trouble and you're the only one who can do anything
about it. The theatre needs new blood.

STONE: (*Scornfully*) There's blood enough in *Hamlet,* my boy. Blood
enough for anyone.

EDMUND: It's getting quite late. Hadn't the set better go up?

JENKINS: (*Belligerently*) Alright, alright! That's all I'm good for around
here!

HELGA: Now, now Jenkins.

EDMUND: For God's sake, let him alone, don't coddle him!

(JENKINS, HELGA, *and* EDMUND *gather up their belongings and exit.*)

ELFIE: Well, Mr. Stone, what do you say?

STONE: Oh, you'll play Ophelia alright. There's no time to rehearse you,
so you'll have to use common sense. (*Calls to* CARL, *who enters in
Hamlet's "customary suit of solemn black" and blond wig.*) Carl, run
through your scene with her, will you? The blocking is a little complicated. If you need me, Carl, I will be in my dressing room. (*Exits.*)

ELFIE: What's blocking?

CARL: It's the plan of all the actors' movements and positions on the stage. Let's run through it. There isn't much time and I have got to get a cup of coffee before the performance tonight. Jenkins, would you run out and get us a couple of cups of coffee?

JENKINS: (*Carrying a ladder across the stage*) Do you want the set to go up or don't you? It's bad enough that I have to go out on a rum-run for your old man. I ain't goin' out for coffee, too. (*Exits.*)

CARL: Sorry I asked.

ELFIE: That fellow's got a chip on his shoulder, hasn't he?

CARL: Never mind the coffee, let's run the scene.

JENKINS: (*Reentering apologetically*) You can have some from my thermos, though.

(ELFIE *and* CARL *exchange a look of surprise.*)

CARL: Why, thank you, Jenkins.

JENKINS: (*Pouring hot coffee into a red thermos cup which they share*) I haven't got any sugar though.

CARL *and* ELFIE: That's alright, I don't take sugar. (*They exchange a look. Then in unison.*) Neither do I.

CARL: (*To* ELFIE) Neither do I.

JENKINS: And it's a good thing you don't. Sugar causes cancer.

CARL: Still eating those health foods, eh Jenkins?

JENKINS: I swear by vegetable juices.

CARL: (*To* ELFIE) Jenkins is a vegetarian.

JENKINS: It's just that I can't stand butchers and butchery. (*Exits.*)

ELFIE: You meet so many interesting people in the theatre.

CARL: Yes.

ELFIE: Oh, this is so exciting! You must love the theatre.

CARL: I am attracted by the theatre, but frankly, I'm repelled by it. I would never have tried to go into the theatre if my parents hadn't been actors. I always wanted to be a marine biologist. The people in the theatre are so insincere; they don't seem to know where the play leaves off and real life begins. And besides, it's not a healthy life. You get a lot of exercise, but at night. I guess that's why acting is called the world's second oldest profession.

ELFIE: Yes, you're cut off from the solar energy. But night is a very intuitive time, don't you think?

CARL: (*Lost in thought, but suddenly coming back to himself*) What? . . . Oh, yes, intuitive.

ELFIE: (*Elbowing him*) Shall we rehearse?

CARL: Oh, we'll be alright but we won't run the risk of getting stale, will we?

ELFIE: Your zeal is only matched by your indifference.

CARL: Your iambics are only surpassed by your pentameters.

ELFIE: Listen, there's one thing about Ophelia I don't feel, ya know what I mean?

CARL: What do you mean?

ELFIE: Is Hamlet mad or only pretending to be?

CARL: He's only pretending.

ELFIE: I don't believe it. If he loves Ophelia, why would he pretend? No, I think he really was mad.

CARL: He wanted to get her out of the way. He was afraid she might get hurt.

ELFIE: And besides, if she really loved him, she would have known that he was not sincere. She would have . . . sensed it.

CARL: Listen, I have watched my father play Hamlet over five hundred times, and I don't know if I'm mad or only pretending to be.

ELFIE: When you act, do you really become the character?

CARL: (*Emphatically*) No, that would be dangerous. Acting is the art of seeming, not being. For instance: I will play Hamlet here tonight. I will seem to be Hamlet. Now, suppose I took a part in another play where I played a character who's playing Hamlet. I would seem to be Hamlet in that play, too. That would be just as good as playing Hamlet, don't you think? Only better. Whatever role we play, we construct it out of our own personalities anyway. We can never be anything other than what we are, so I say to seem is better than to be.

ELFIE: I see. To be an actress or not to be an actress . . . to ruin one's life before a room full of people. What fun!

CARL: (*Rashly*) Besides, Hamlet was a great actor.

ELFIE: And she was just a green ingenue.

CARL: A green ingenue . . . sounds like a sauce.

ELFIE: Listen. There's something I've always wanted to know about acting. When you have to cry onstage, actually produce real tears, night after night, how do you do it? Do you provoke the pain externally by pinching yourself where nobody can see? Or do you endow the situation with sense memory? Once I read in Uta Hagen's book that instead of concentrating on producing real tears, which would make you lose the value of the scene, what you should do is invoke a poetic image that would bring tears to your eyes, like a lonely, frail, delicate tree in the middle of a vast, windy prairie.

CARL: Throughout the great ages of the theatre, the greatest actors of every generation have, well, uh . . . my mother always did it this way. (*Grabs a kleenex from the dressing table and begins to cry violently.*)

ELFIE: (*Amazed*) Real tears!

CARL: Would you like to try it?

ELFIE: Yes!

CARL: Take this onion, take this handkerchief. Now, holding the handkerchief in the right hand and the onion in the left (of course, if you're facing in the other direction, it's all reversed, but we'll get to that). Now, the handkerchief is like a little stage curtain, concealing the onion from the audience's view. It goes up and comes down, see? Up and down. Of course the great Berma was reputed to have been able to hold the onion and the handkerchief in one hand, but I think that's too advanced for you. We'll just take it one step at a time. Forget the play, the scene, the character, just go for the eternal thing; go for the emotion. Work yourself up.

(ELFIE *begins to cry.*)

CARL: (*Coaching her on*) Get upset . . . get more upset. Lower your head . . . Squeeze a little onion juice in your eye. That's it. (*Pointing to a tear on her cheek.*) There it is! A little one, but it's a beginning. You were beautiful. You were . . . beautiful! You may keep the onion if you wish.

ELFIE: I'll treasure it always. I wish I could be right for you. I wish I could be thirty-five, have my hair bleached, and say sophisticated things.

CARL: Promise me something, Elfie.

ELFIE: What?

CARL: That you'll never say sophisticated things, never have your hair bleached, and never ever be thirty-five.

(*They kiss.*)

JENKINS: (*Interrupting*) Do you know that half hour was called fifteen minutes ago?

CARL: Come. On to the dressing room. I hope you're the type that can wear any size.

ELFIE: What shall I take as a stage name?

CARL: How about Irving?

STONE: (*Overhearing as he enters in Ghost costume*) Ah, yes, Irving. I used to fetch his ale when I was pump boy at the Old Beefsteak Club Room.

CARL: Pop is a member . . .

STONE: In good standing . . .

CARL: In good standing of the Sublime Society of Beefsteaks!

STONE: Of which Sheridan was a member. I want you to understand one thing, Miss Fey. Our company may be small but it's pretentious.

JENKINS: (*Entering*) Will you three please get off the stage? It's time to let the audience in.

STONE: This is going to be a great performance. I feel inspired. Miss Fey, you have inspired me.

(*Exeunt omnes. There is a change of light and the sounds of an audience heard over Elizabethan music. The curtain rises on Act I, Scene I of the Caucasian Theatrical Company's production of* Hamlet. *Elsinore. Fog on the battlements. A banshee wails.*)

EDMUND: Who's there?

HELGA: Nay, answer me. Stand and unfold yourself.

EDMUND: Long live the king!

HELGA: Bernardo?

EDMUND: He.

HELGA: You come most carefully upon your hour.

(*They shake hands.* EDMUND *has a buzzer concealed in his palm and gives* HELGA *a shock.*)

HELGA: (*Under her breath*) You damn practical joker!

EDMUND: 'Tis now struck twelve. Get thee to bed, Francisco.

HELGA: For this relief much thanks. 'Tis bitter cold, and I am sick at heart.

EDMUND: Have you had quiet guard?

HELGA: Not a mouse stirring.

EDMUND: Well, good night.
    If you do meet Hamlet and Horatio,
    The rivals of my watch, bid them make haste.

(*Enter* CARL *and* JENKINS.)

HELGA: I think I hear them. Stand, ho! Who is there?

JENKINS: Friends to this ground.

CARL: And liegemen to the Dane.

HELGA: Give you good night.

JENKINS: O, farewell, honest soldier. Who hath relieved you?

HELGA: Bernardo hath my place. Give you good night. (*Exits.*)

CARL: The air bites shrewdly; it is very cold.

JENKINS: It is a nipping and an eager air.

CARL: What hour now?

JENKINS: I think it lacks of twelve.

EDMUND: No, it is struck.

JENKINS: Indeed? I heard it not. It then draws near the season wherein the spirit held his wont to walk. (*Ghost enters.*) Look, my lord, it comes.

CARL: Angels and ministers of grace defend us!
   Be thou a spirit of health or goblin damned,
   Bring with thee airs from heaven or blasts from hell,
   Be thy intents wicked or charitable,
   Thou com'st in such a questionable shape
   That I will speak to thee. I'll call thee Hamlet,
   King, father, royal Dane. O, answer me!
   Let me not burst in ignorance, but tell
   Why thy canonized bones, hearsed in death,
   Have burst their cerements, why the sepulchre
   Wherein we saw thee quietly interred
   Hath oped his ponderous and marble jaws
   To cast thee up again. What may this mean
   That thou, dead corpse, again in complete steel,
   Revisits thus the glimpses of the moon,
   Making night hideous, and we fools of nature
   So horridly to shake our disposition
   With thoughts beyond the reaches of our souls?
   Say, why is this? Wherefore?
   What should we do?

(*Ghost beckons.*)

JENKINS: It beckons you to go away with it,
   As if it some impartment did desire
   To you alone.
EDMUND: Look with what courteous action
   It waves you to a more removed ground.
   But do not go with it.
JENKINS: Do not, my lord.
CARL: Why, what should be the fear?
   I do not set my life at a pin's fee,
   And for my soul, what can it do to that,
   Being a thing immortal as itself?

It waves me forth again. I'll follow it.

JENKINS: What if it tempt you toward the flood, my lord.
Or to the dreadful summit of the cliff
That beetles o'er his base into the sea,
And there assume some other horrible form,
Which might deprive your sovereignty of reason
And draw you into madness? Think of it.
The very place puts toys of desperation,
Without more motive, into every brain
That looks so many fathoms to the sea
And hears it roar beneath.

CARL: It waves me still.
Go on. I'll follow thee.

EDMUND: You shall not go, my lord.

CARL: Hold off your hands.

JENKINS: Be ruled. You shall not go.

CARL: My fate cries out
And makes each petty artery in this body
As hardy as the Nemean lion's nerve.
Still am I called. Unhand me, gentlemen.
By heaven, I'll make a ghost of him that lets me!
I say, away! Go on. I'll follow thee.

(*Exit Ghost and Hamlet.*)

JENKINS: He waxes desperate with imagination.

EDMUND: Let's follow. 'Tis not fit thus to obey him.

JENKINS: Have after. To what issue will this come?

EDMUND: Something is denten in the state of Rotmark. O, shit!

(*A blood-curdling scream is heard. All run into the dressing room.* HEL-GA *stands with blood on her hand, screaming.* STONE *lies dead, his head in the toilet, blood issuing from his ear.*)

CARL: (*Coming in*) What is it? What's happened? Omigod, it's Pop!

Charles Ludlam

HELGA: (*In shock*) At first I thought it was real. Then I saw it was only stage blood!

CARL: He's dead.

HELGA: It isn't real. It's stage blood, I tell you! Stage blood!

(*Curtain. End of Act I.*)

ACT II

Scene: Same as in Act I. HELGA *sits at the dressing table removing her makeup.* EDMUND *is seated on the toilet, upstage.*

EDMUND: (*Reading* Variety) Pap, pap, nothing but pap. (*Finishes, attempts to flush.*) This damn toilet never works.

HELGA: I'll have Carl take a look at it. He's real good with the W.C.

EDMUND: (*Begins to shave*) What does your Ouija board say now, Helga?

HELGA: All that is I see.

EDMUND: You're going to go up in your lines tonight?

HELGA: Yeah, Ouija doesn't play favorites.

(*She opens a jar of cold cream and a snake jumps out at her. She screams.*)

(Affectionately.) You damn practical joker.

EDMUND: (*Referring to Ouija board*) Why don't you ask it who killed the old man?

HELGA: Who do you think killed him?

EDMUND: I think you did it.

HELGA: (*Laughing gaily*) Of course I did it . . . to get the company for you, my baby.

(HELGA *embraces and kisses* EDMUND, *whose face is covered with shaving cream.*)

EDMUND: Oh, come on, right here!

HELGA: No!

EDMUND: There's plenty of time . . . I've been a bad boy today, Mamma.

HELGA: Edmund's been a bad boy.

(*He drops his pants. She playfully whips him with his belt.*)

EDMUND: I'm gonna get you, Mamma.

HELGA: He's after me!

EDMUND: (*Grabs her fur coat and throws it over them*) Venus in furs!

CARL: (*Calling from offstage*) Mother! Mother!

HELGA: (*Startled*) Oh, my God, it's Carl! He'll be here any minute.

(*They jump up.* EDMUND *grabs his clothes and tries to put on his pants.*)

EDMUND: Tell him you've had enough. You're fed up. Lay down the law. Do you want *him* to manage this company or *me?*

HELGA: You, of course, darling. (*Kisses him.*)

EDMUND: What are you going to tell him?

CARL: (*Off*) Mother?

HELGA: Don't worry about me. Hide. He'll be here any minute.

(EDMUND *hides behind the arras.* CARL *enters, goes to the toilet, to urinate.*)

CARL: Toilet not working?

HELGA: Yeah. Would you have a look at it?

CARL: I'll fix it. (*Does so.*)

HELGA: Now, Carl, what's the matter?

CARL: I want to run some lines from the closet scene.

HELGA: Must we? This day has just exhausted me.

CARL: It seems so cold-blooded. This morning we buried Pop, this afternoon we've replaced him, and tonight we're going on.

HELGA: We must perform. There is no posthumous fame for actors.

JENKINS: (*Poking in his head*) Carl, there's a man out front who wants to see you.

CARL: Who is it?

JENKINS: He looks like a mortician's bill collector, if you ask me.

HELGA: You can't get much lower than that.

CARL: (*To* HELGA) Alright, we won't rehearse. (*To* JENKINS.) Send him in. (*Exit* JENKINS.)

HELGA: I'm going to see about supper.

CARL: Mother, there's something I want to discuss with you.

HELGA: What is it?

CARL: Mother, I think Pop was murdered.

HELGA: Carl, I don't want to talk about this. It was suicide. He was all washed up. He couldn't take the humiliation of playing his hometown.

CARL: Someone we know did it. Someone in this company.

HELGA: Carl, you're frightening me.

CARL: Perhaps a little fear would do you good. Someone in this company killed my father and I'm not going to rest until I find out who it is.

HELGA: You look tired.

CARL: I can't think about that now. There's the performance tonight, and later I've got to go over all the books. Pop always took care of the business end, and I guess now it's up to me. There are a lot of bills to be paid; death is expensive.

HELGA: Carl, I think you're working too hard. You shouldn't have to think about money. You need to concentrate on playing Hamlet just now. Why don't we get someone else to take care of the dull business end of it? Then you'd have more time to think about your art . . .

(*A small crash is heard off.*)

CARL: (*Suddenly starting to his feet, draws prop sword*) What's that! A rat! (*Stabs sword through the costume rack, as if it were the arras in the closet scene of* Hamlet.) Dead for a ducat! Dead!

HELGA: (*Shrieks*) Don't!

CARL: (*Diving through the costume rack*) There's no one there!

(*The door to the dressing room, stage left, opens and* EDMUND *falls in dead, with a dagger stuck in his back.* HELGA *and* CARL *turn and gasp.* EDMUND *jumps up laughing, and pulls the dagger out of his back.*)

EDMUND Ha! Ha! Ha! Cute trick don't you think? I had Jenkins order it.

CARL: *You* had Jenkins order it?!

EDMUND: Yes, the blade retracts into the handle. We should try it out tonight, don't you think?

HELGA: Carl, Edmund has a lot of ideas about how we can improve the company.

EDMUND: Yes, Carl, I'm going to handle the management from now on.

CARL: You? (*Laughing.*) Mother, did you hear that?

HELGA: It's true, Carl. Edmund and I are going to be married.

CARL: (*Retching*) Mother! A beast that wants discourse of reason would have mourned longer.

HELGA: Now, Carl, don't get all excited. It'll just spoil your performance.

CARL: It didn't hurt your performance (*makes obscene gestures*), did it, Edmund?

EDMUND: Your sense of humor and mine differ.

CARL: Well, if you don't like it, get out of my dressing room, mother-fucker!

(*They go to fight,* HELGA *comes between them.*)

GILBERT: (*Entering*) Oh, excuse me, I'm interrupting.

HELGA: Not at all. We were just leaving. (*Pushes* EDMUND *through the door and following, turns to* CARL.) Carl, try to understand. (*Then looking* GILBERT *up and down.*) Exactly like a mortician's bill collector. (*Exits.*)

GILBERT: You don't know me, Mr. Stone. My name is Fey, Gilbert Fey. I'm Elfie's father.

CARL: What can I do for you?

GILBERT: Prevent my daughter from going on the stage.

CARL: Isn't that up to her?

GILBERT: It most certainly is not. She's underage. If she leaves with you on tour, I'll slap you with statutory rape.

CARL: Your threats don't frighten me, Mr. Fey. She's your daughter, you control her.

GILBERT: If only I could. She's strong-willed and once they get a taste of the theatre, there's no reasoning with them.

CARL: Your daughter is an inspired actress.

GILBERT: I know that I may be wasting my time appealing to the honor of an immoral actor, but I do appeal to that honor in the hope that it exists. Please help me.

CARL: As you just pointed out, you have the law on your side. What do you need me for?

GILBERT: Ah, if only it were as simple as that.

CARL: You see this bottle?

GILBERT: Stage blood?

CARL: Yeah, stage blood. It's not real blood; it's the blood we use on-stage. That's what your daughter has in her veins.

GILBERT: You are an actor; disillusion her. She must not go the way Carlton went.

CARL: Carlton? What do you know about my father?

GILBERT: I'll make a deal with you. Stop my daughter's career and I'll tell you who killed your father.

CARL: It's a deal. On one condition: that you let her finish the performance tonight. You see, we don't have an Ophelia.

GILBERT; Ah, that sounds dangerous.

CARL: Mr. Fey . . . a moment ago you called me an immoral actor. Frankly, I was shocked. Now I see that perhaps what you say may be true. The theatre is my church. To act my experience of God. But I only have one scruple: to get the play onto the stage. Because I sacrifice myself to that end, I do not flinch at sacrificing others. Let your daughter play Ophelia tonight, and I promise that I will send her back to you, a little shaken perhaps, but cured of the theatre forever.

GILBERT: Thank you.

CARL: But I warn you, I shall have to hurt her. Perhaps even subject her to some humiliation.

GILBERT: Yes, hurt her, if you must. But cure her of this thing, this stage blood.

CARL: Consider her cured.

GILBERT: (*Starts to go, stops and turns*) What if she doesn't believe you?

CARL: Don't worry about that, Mr. Fey. Those of us who make our livings at make-believe are the most easily taken in by it.

GILBERT: (*Smiling an oily smile and taking his wallet out of his inside jacket pocket*) May I offer some remuneration for what may be your greatest performance?

CARL: (*Snatching money*) Now get out before I throw you out!

(FEY *beats a hasty retreat.* JENKINS *enters with a toilet brush and scrubs toilet bowl, whistling while he cleans.*)

CARL: (*To* JENKINS) You're going to have to play the ghost tonight. I don't know what you're going to do for armor.

JENKINS: (*Still scrubbing bloody toilet*) I just happen to have a suit that fits me.

CARL: That fits you???

JENKINS: (*In cold blood*) Yeah, I always had a feeling I was going to play that part some day.

CARL: But you knew Pop would only let you play it over his dead body.

(*Pregnant pause.*)

JENKINS: It wasn't me. But I think I do know who killed your old man. (*Starts to leave, then turning and coming toward* CARL.) And I'm going to tell you after tonight's performance.

(A *sandbag falls from the flies just outside of the door and crashes to the floor of the stage, missing* JENKINS *by inches.*)

CARL: A sandbag! Jenkins, if I've told you once, I've told you a thousand times, never whistle in the dressing room. It's bad luck! Unless you say a line from *Hamlet* immediately afterward. Now go get into costume. And Jenkins, when you hear that call: "Places"—you know that you're going on because if you're not, you're in the wrong business.

We've got a performance to give, and you're on in the first act. Now
go on . . . and Jenkins, break a leg. (JENKINS *exits hurriedly, trips over
the sandbag, and falls.*)

JENKINS: "He smote the sledded Polacks on the ice."

CARL: Are you sure that's from *Hamlet?*

JENKINS: Yes, it's from Horatio's first ghost scene. They always cut it.

CARL: No wonder. I never thought that Shakespeare would stoop to a
Polish joke! (JENKINS *exits.*)

CARL: (*Alone, changing from* CARL *to Hamlet*) A father is a necessary
evil. Shakespeare must have written *Hamlet* in the months following his father's death. Fatherhood in the sense of conscious beget-
ting is entirely unknown to man. From only begetter to only be-
gotten. For all we know, fatherhood may be a legal fiction. Who is
the father of any son that any son should love him? The son un-
born mars his mother's beauty; born he brings pain, divides affection, increases care. He is a male: his growth his father's decline,
his youth his father's envy, his friend his father's enemy. (*Regard-
ing his nude body in the mirror.*) Oh, that this too too solid flesh
would melt.

JENKINS: (*Off*) Hamlet, I am thy father's spirit.

CARL: (*Startled*) Oh, it's Jenkins rehearsing.

STONE'S VOICE: You are the dispossessed son: I am the murdered father:
your mother is the guilty queen.

(*Enter* GHOST *as in* Hamlet. *He speaks in* STONE, SR.*'s voice.*)

CARL: I can't believe my eyes.

GHOST: To my son I speak. The son of my soul.
The son of my body.
My son! and what's a son?
A thing begot within a pair of minutes, there about;
A lump bred up in darkness, and doth serve
To balance those light creatures we call women;
And at the nine months' end creeps forth to light.
What is there yet in a son,

To make a father dote, rave or run mad?
Being born, it pouts, cries, and breeds teeth.
What is there yet in a son?
He must be fed, be taught to go, and speak.
Ay, or yet? Why might not a man love a calf as well?
Or melt in passion o'er a frisking kid, as for a son?
Methinks a young bacon,
Or a fine little smooth horse colt,
Should move a man as much as doth a son;
For one of these, in very little time,
Will grow to some good use; whereas a son,
The more he grows in stature and in years,
The more unsquared, unlevel'd he appears;
Reckons his parents among the rank of fools,
Strikes cares upon their heads with his mad riots,
Makes them look old before they meet with age:
This is a son.

CARL: Art thou there truepenny?

GHOST: I died so that my namesake may live forever. My brother didn't do it. My brother didn't do it.

CARL: I never thought he did!

GHOST: Man at ten is any animal, at twenty a lunatic, at thirty a failure, at forty a fraud, at fifty a criminal. Damn good gin that was!

CARL: (*Applauds*) Father! A masterly rendition.

(*The* GHOST *disappears.*)

HELGA: (*Off*) Carl . . . Carl. (*Enters.*) Carl, you're not dressed yet . . . and you're on in five minutes!

(*She frantically helps him dress.*)

CARL: All these hooks and eyes . . . I'll never make it . . . Why can't we get any tights that fit?

HELGA: You're not in New York now, darling, this is Mudville. Carl, why don't you get one of your tricks to do your sewing for you?

CARL: It's so hard to meet anyone on the road, Mother.

HELGA: Tell me about it.

CARL: It could be worse, Mother. We could be in Vienna.

HELGA: Carl, I told you never to mention Vienna to me again.

CARL: Slowly I turn and inch by inch, step by step . . .

HELGA: Ah, Vienna, the city of my nightmares. The only town we played where we had to go back to our hotel rooms to take a piss.

CARL: What about the night that Edmund Dundreary was discovered in his hotel room forcing a load of shit down the sink with his thumb? He couldn't find the key to the W.C. in the middle of the night.

HELGA: Jenkins never got over it.

CARL: I never got over it.

HELGA: Vienna never got over it. Carl, haven't you forgotten something?

CARL: Oh, yes, the locket.

HELGA: (Holds up wig) Carl . . .

CARL: No! Not the wig.

HELGA: Carl, you've got to wear the wig.

CARL: Mother, if I've told you once I've told you a hundred times: I hate that wig!

HELGA: Carl, you have to wear the wig!

CARL: People laugh at me when I come onstage in that wig.

HELGA: Go with it, go with it! Carl, please, you cannot play Hamlet without being blond. It's never been done in theatre before.

CARL: Well, why not? Some Danes have black hair.

HELGA: Name five. Please, Carl, wear the wig. (In baby talk:) Wear the wiggie, wiggie, wiggie. (CARL resists.) Please, Carl, don't make me beg. (She begins crying. He gives in and takes the wig.) Thank you. And tonight could you true up the "to be or not to be" speech? It's been a little too two-dimensional. Try to mean what you are saying. No wooden Hamlets. Not even in the sticks. (Exits.)

CARL: Yes, Mother. Why, I know the "to be or not to be" speech so well that I could say it backwards. "Question the is that; be to not or, be

To." (*He enters the playing area as Hamlet and begins the "To be or not to be" speech.*)
To be, or not to be . . .
(*Whispers.*) Line!
That is the question.
Whether 'tis nobler in the mind to suffer
The slings and arrows of outrageous fortune,
Or to take arms against a sea of troubles
And by opposing end them. To die, to sleep—
No more, and by a sleep to say we end
The heartache and the thousand natural shocks
That flesh is heir to. 'Tis a consummation
Devoutly to be wished. To die, to sleep,
To sleep—perchance to dream. Aye, there's the rub,
For in that sleep of death what dreams may come
When we have shuffled off this mortal coil
Must give us pause. There's the respect
That makes calamity of so long life.
For who would bear the whips and scorns of time,
The oppressor's wrong, the proud man's contumely
The pangs of despised love, the law's delay,
The insolence of office and the spurns
That patient merit of the unworthy takes,
When he himself might his quietus make
With bare bodkin? Who would fardels bear,
To grunt and sweat under a weary life,
But that the dread of something after death,
The undiscovered country from whose bourn
No traveler returns, puzzles the will,
And makes us rather bear those ills we have
Than fly to others that we know not of?
Thus conscience does make cowards of us all,
And thus the native hue of resolution
Is sicklied o'er with the pale cast of thought,

And enterprises of great pitch and moment
With this regard their currents turn awry
And lose the name of action.—Soft you now!
The fair Ophelia! Nymph, in thy orisons
Be all my sins remembered.

(*Enter* ELFIE *as Ophelia.*)

ELFIE: Good my lord,
How does your honor for this many a day?
CARL: I humbly thank you, well, well, well.
ELFIE: My lord, I have remembrances of yours
That I have longed long to redeliver.
I pray you, now receive them.
CARL: No, not I,
I never gave you aught.
ELFIE: My honored lord, you know right well you did,
And with them words of so sweet breath composed
As made the things more rich. Their perfume lost,
Take these again, for to the noble mind
Rich gifts wax poor when givers prove unkind.
There, my lord.
CARL: Are you honest?
ELFIE: My lord?
CARL: Are you fair?
ELFIE: What means your lordship?
CARL: That if you be honest and fair, your honesty should admit no discourse to your beauty.
ELFIE: Could beauty, my lord, have better commerce than with honesty?
CARL: Ay, truly, for the power of beauty will sooner transform honesty from what it is to a bawd than the force of honesty can translate beauty into his likeness. This was sometime a paradox, but now the time gives it proof.

(HELGA *and* EDMUND *enter watching from the wings, dressed as Gertrude and Claudius.*)

EDMUND: (*To* HELGA) We almost muffed it in that last little scene.

HELGA: I'm afraid that Carl is going to be trouble.

EDMUND: You can handle him. Use a little psychology.

HELGA: That's underhanded, Edmund. I wouldn't stoop to using psychology.

(ELFIE *and* CARL *continue the performance of* Hamlet.)

CARL: I did love you once.

ELFIE: Indeed, my lord, you made me believe so.

CARL: (*Seeing his mother and* EDMUND *kissing in the wings*)
You should not have believed me, for virtue cannot
So innoculate our old stock but we shall
Relish of it. I loved you not.

ELFIE: I was the more deceived.

CARL: Get thee to a nunnery. Why wouldst thou be a breeder of sinners? I am myself indifferent honest, but yet I could accuse me of such things that it were better my mother had not borne me: I am very proud, revengeful, ambitious, with more offenses at my beck than I have thoughts to put them in, imagination to give them shape, or time to act them in. What should such fellows as I do crawling between earth and heaven? We are arrant knaves all; believe none of us. Go thy ways to a nunnery.

ELFIE: O, help him, you sweet heavens!

EDMUND: She's good, really good.

HELGA: She even makes *him* look good.

CARL: (*As* Hamlet) I have heard of your paintings too, well enough. God hath given you one face, and you make yourselves another. You jig, you amble, and you lisp; you nickname God's creatures and make your wantonness your ignorance. Go to, I'll no more on't; it hath made me mad. I say we will have no more marriage. Those that are married—all but one—shall live. The rest shall keep as they are. To a nunnery, go.

(*Applause is heard.* CARL *exits from the stage through the arras to the dressing room. We hear* ELFIE *as Ophelia finishing the scene with her lament through the curtain.*)

ELFIE: O, what a noble mind is here o'erthrown!
 The courtier's, soldier's, scholar's, eye, tongue, sword,
 Th' expectancy and rose of the fair state,
 The glass of fashion and the mold of form,
 Th' observed of all observers, quite, quite down!
 And I, of ladies most deject and wretched,
 That sucked the honey of his musicked vows,
 Now see that noble and most sovereign reason
 Like sweet bells jangled, out of time and harsh,
 That unmatched form and feature of blown youth
 Blasted with ecstasy, O, woe is me
 T'have seen what I have seen, see what I see!

(*During* ELFIE'S *speech,* JENKINS *and* CARL *are in the dressing room.*)

JENKINS: (*Handing* CARL *a whiskey bottle half full*) Here's the whiskey bottle you wanted. I found it in the prop room.
CARL: I'll empty it. Do you have some tea?
JENKINS: That's tea in it now. I know you don't drink.
CARL: (*Sniffs it*) Tea!
JENKINS: Rose hip . . . organic . . . vitamin C.
CARL: Thank you, Jenkins, you're my right arm.
JENKINS: But, tell me, what scene are you going to use it in?
CARL: In a little scene I'm going to play right now. (*Both listening to last of* ELFIE'S *speech.*) Leave me alone with her.
JENKINS: What are you going to do?
CARL: That's between the Father, the Son, and the Holy Ghost.

JENKINS: P.U. All religion stinks to . . .

CARL: High heaven? Yes, I know.

(JENKINS *heaves a sign and exits.* ELFIE *enters dressing room.* CARL *is sitting at dressing table drinking.*)

ELFIE: Carl, is something wrong?

CARL: Why do you ask?

ELFIE: (*Troubled, perhaps even haunted*) There was something about your eyes . . . I don't know. Maybe it was just my imagination, but you looked as though you were going to tear my clothes off me. It frightened me.

CARL: Tear your clothes off you? (*He drinks from the bottle.*)

ELFIE: (*Shocked*) Carl, you're not drinking? (*Trying to reason with him.*) You should smoke grass, dear. That stuff will ruin your liver.

CARL: (*Brash, almost obnoxious*) Of course, I'm drinking. I'm an actor, not a goddamn hippie! The drama originated as a festival of Dionysus. (*Ranting.*) Grapes! Wine! Intoxication!

ELFIE: Please stop drinking! You have a performance to give.

CARL: That's one of the highly guarded secrets of our profession. All actors are better drunk. (*Belches.*)

ELFIE: That's disgusting!

CARL: What's disgusting about it? It's more constructive than what most people do when they're drunk.

ELFIE: Here, take back your rabbit's foot.

CARL: I never gave that to you.

ELFIE: You did, but take it back. For to the noble mind, rich gifts wax poor when givers prove unkind.

CARL: (*Sarcastically*) I saw the movie.

ELFIE: Carl, I know that you're going through something terrible about your father. But I'll stand by you. I'd do anything for you.

CARL: (*Rubbing her face with his hand*) What's that on your face?

ELFIE: Makeup. I'm an actress now.

CARL: What do you need makeup for? What's wrong with your own face?

(*He splashes her face with water and wipes it clean. Then he kisses her.*)

ELFIE: (*Aroused*) Carl, do you know how you make me feel?

CARL: (*Shocked at her willingness*) No, I don't know how I make you feel, but I know how you look—like a whore! (*Spanks her.*)

ELFIE: (*Outraged*) I hate you and I hate the theatre! I'll do Jenkins' studio performance tonight but, after that, I never want to see you or the inside of a theatre again. (*Exits.*)

CARL: Don't slam the door. (*Sound of door slamming and applause.*)

(FEY *enters.*)

GILBERT: Well played, Mr. Stone. You've kept your part of the bargain.

CARL: And now, Mr. Fey, you keep your part of the bargain. Who did it, Mr. Fey? Who was the dirty rat who killed my father?

GILBERT: I killed him.

CARL: You!!!

GILBERT: Look at my face . . . over here in the light.

CARL: Omigod!

GILBERT: You see a resemblance? Yes, I killed Carlton and I impersonated the Ghost . . . We were twins, Carlton and I, and we were both stage-struck.

CARL: Then you're my . . .

GILBERT: Yes, I'm your Uncle Gilbert.

CARL: You killed your own brother to indulge a petty jealousy?

GILBERT: Yes, yes. It should be easy for you to understand. It's in my veins too—this stage blood.

CARL: You killed your own brother to play his role for one night?!

GILBERT: You'd let me fry for that, wouldn't you? But, there's more to it than that, believe me. Hear me out. Percy and me . . . yes, that was your old man's name before he changed it for the stage—Percy Fey . . .

CARL: (*Shocked*) You mean my name isn't Stone?

GILBERT: No, it's Fey, Raymond Fey.

CARL: Ray Fey! Omigod! It's horrible!

GILBERT: Percy got a local girl in trouble, and she bore his baby in a wood-shed. Percy didn't want the little bastard to saddle him with responsibility, so he seized the child and tried to drown it in a drunken scene. I beat on him and saved the child. He ran away that night with a road show and never came back. I made that girl an honest woman, and raised his child . . . Elfie Fey.

CARL: Then she's my sister!

GILBERT: She's your half sister.

CARL: He might have killed Elfie. Still, revenge cannot be justified.

GILBERT: Then you mean you'll let me fry, after all? But whatever course of action you choose to take, never let her know that that foul, old drunken piece of human garbage . . . God rest his soul . . . was her father.

CARL: Uncle Gilbert, you'll find that blood is thicker than water, especially stage blood . . . Uncle Gilbert, do you think you could memorize a short speech of about twenty lines? You see, Elfie and I are doing a scene from Jenkins' experimental drama, *Fossil Fuel.* We're trying to convince Mother that it might be profitable to add an avant-garde play to the repertoire. And I think we might just have a part in it for you.

GILBERT: Oh, I'd be honored to play with you, Mr. Stone.

CARL: Come back tonight after the performance, and I'll have the whole thing written out for you.

GILBERT: Aye, my lord. (*Exits.*)

EDMUND: (*Entering dressing room*) Carl, your mother wants to see you.

CARL: You say my mother?

EDMUND: She wants to speak with you in her dressing room before the closet scene.

CARL: Tell her I'll obey. Were she ten times our mother!

(CARL *puts on a wig and enters the* Hamlet *stage where* HELGA *as Gertrude awaits him.* FEY *sneaks into the dressing room during the following scene; he snoops around, takes a sip from the fake bottle of booze, spits it out, then eavesdrops by the arras.*)

CARL: Now, Mother, what's the matter?

HELGA: Hamlet, thou hast thy father much offended.

CARL: Mother, you have my father much offended.

HELGA: Come, come, you answer with an idle tongue.

CARL: Go, go, you question with a wicked tongue.

HELGA: Why, how now, Hamlet?

CARL: What's the matter now?

HELGA: Have you forgot me?

(*Weeps. An onion drops from* HELGA's *handkerchief.*)

CARL: No, by the rood, not so!
   You are the Queen, your husband's brother's wife,
   And, would it were not so, you are my mother.

HELGA: Nay, then I'll set those to you that can speak.

CARL: Come, come, and sit you down. You shall not budge.
   You go not till I set you up a glass
   Where you may see the inmost part of you.

HELGA: What wilt thou do? Thou wilt not murder me? Help, ho!

GILBERT: What, ho! Help!

CARL: (*Draws*) What's that? A rat? Dead for a ducat, dead! (*Makes a pass
   through the arras.*)

GILBERT: O, I am slain.

HELGA: O me, what hast thou done?

CARL: Nay, I know not. Is it the King?

HELGA: O, what a rash and bloody deed is this!

CARL: A bloody deed—almost as bad, good mother,
   As kill a king, and marry with his brother.

HELGA: As kill a king?

CARL: Ay, lady, it was my word.

(*Lifts up the arras and sees that he has accidentally killed* GILBERT.)

Uncle Gilbert?
Thou wretched, rash, intruding fool, farewell!
I took thee for thy better. Take thy fortune.

Thou find'st to be too busy is some danger.—
Leave wringing of your hands. Peace, sit you down
And let me wring your heart,
If it be made of penetrable stuff.
If damned custom have not brazed it so
That it be proof and bulwark against sense.
HELGA: What have I done that thou dar'st wag thy tongue
In noise so rude against me?
CARL: Look here upon this picture, and on this,
The counterfeit presentment of two brothers.
This was your husband. Look you now what follows.
HELGA: O Hamlet, speak no more.
Thou turn'st mine eyes into my very soul.
And there I see such black and grained spots.
As will not leave their tinct.
CARL: Nay, but to live
In the rank sweat of an enseamed bed,
Stewed in corruption, honeying and making love
Over the nasty sty—
HELGA: O, speak to me no more.
These words like daggers enter in mine ears.
No more, sweet Hamlet.
CARL: A murderer and a villain,
A slave that is not twentieth part the tithe
Of your precedent lord, a vice of kings,
A cutpurse of the empire and the rule,
That from a shelf the precious diadem stole
And put it in his pocket—
HELGA: No more.

(*Enter* GHOST.)

CARL: A king of shreds and patches—
Save me and hover o'er me with your wings,
You heavenly guards? What would your gracious figure?

Charles Ludlam

HELGA: Alas, he's mad.

CARL: Do you not come your tardy son to chide,
    That lapsed in time and passion, lets go by
    Th' important acting of your dread command?
    O, say!

GHOST: Do not forget. This visitation
    Is but to whet thy almost blunted purpose.
    But look, amazement on thy mother sits.
    O, step between her and her fighting soul!
    Conceit in weakest bodies strongest works.
    Speak to her, Hamlet.

CARL: How is it with you, lady?

HELGA: Alas, how is't with you,
    That you do bend your eye on vacancy,
    And with th' incorporal air do hold discourse?
    Forth at your eyes your spirits wildly peep,
    And as the sleeping soldiers in th' alarm
    Your bedded hairs like life in excrements
    Start up and stand on end. O gentle son,
    Upon the heat and flame of thy distemper
    Sprinkle cool patience. Whereon do you look?

CARL: On him, on him! Look you, how pale he glares!
    His form and cause conjoined, preaching to stones,
    Would make them capable.—Do not look upon me,
    Lest with this piteous action you convert
    My stern effects. Then what I have to do
    Will want true color; tears perchance for blood.

(A second Ghost enters; pushes the first off the edge of the stage, and
    exits hurriedly pursued by the first.)

HELGA: To whom do you speak this?

CARL: Do you see nothing there?

HELGA: Nothing at all; yet all that is I see.

CARL: Nor did you nothing hear?

HELGA: No, nothing but ourselves.

CARL: Why, look you there! Look how it steals away!
　　My father, in his habit as he lived!
　　Look where he goes even now out at the portal!

(*Exit* CARL, *chasing the Ghosts out of the theatre.*)

HELGA: This is the very coinage of your brain.
　　This bodiless creation ecstasy
　　Is very cunning in.

CARL: Ecstasy!!!

(*Blackout. All the characters in the play grope about the stage, in the darkness, carrying lighted candles.*)

JENKINS: (*Announcing*) Ladies and Gentlemen, please stand by. Remain seated. A fuse has blown.

HELGA: (*Voice in the dark*) What's the matter?

JENKINS: There's a short circuit.

HELGA: Call wardrobe and have it lengthened. (*If the audience moans,* HELGA *says, "Did you people come here for entertainment or revenge?"*)

VOICE OF OPEHLIA: Alas, he's mad!

HELGA: Behind the arras, hearing something stir, whips out his rapier, and cries, "A rat, a rat," and in his brainish apprehension kills the unseen, good old man.

EDMUND: O, heavy deed!

HELGA: Your wisdom best shall think.

EDMUND: It shall be so. Madness in great ones must not unwatched go.

(*Suddenly the lights come up on* CARL.)

CARL: Jenkins, Jenkins!

JENKINS: (*Entering*) Carl! I dug up this skull in the prop room last night. It's real!

CARL: (*Taking the skull*) Alas! Poor Urine. He pissed his life away.

JENKINS: Carl, that skull belonged to the stage manager of the Walnut St. Theatre.

CARL: In Philadelphia?

JENKINS: Yeah. He had seen Edwin Booth play Hamlet countless times, so, when he died, he willed his skull to the theatre, to be scraped out and bleached and used in productions of *Hamlet.*

CARL: Jenkins, why don't you do that?

JENKINS: I've donated my body to science, but I guess they could send over the head.

CARL: Jenkins, what did you say this stage manager's name was?

JENKINS: Bernard . . .

CARL: Not Bernard Waxberger?

JENKINS: Bernard Waxberger!

CARL: I knew him, Jenkins! Why, you'd never know to look at him now, but he had quite a sense of humor. Many a time while Pop was trampling the boards as Hamlet, he'd carry me piggyback through the flies. You know, he knew all the minor roles in Shakespeare's plays.

JENKINS: They're the most difficult.

CARL: Of course. Everybody knows that. Whenever a road company came in with a skeletal cast, he'd just fill in. He was reputed to have been the greatest Osric who ever lived. . . . Jenkins, I read your play last night. All eighteen hundred pages of it. It's good! Really good. You've got something there.

JENKINS: You read it?

CARL: That scene where the woman is tied to a railroad track is really suspenseful.

JENKINS: That may not be good. I want to keep the emotional tone low-key. An author must look on murder and mutilation with a dispassionate eye. You see, I cannot show the inner workings of the murderer's mind. I must not. For the identity of the murderer is kept hidden until the end of the play . . . Carl, I've thought it ever since this morning. Karen killed your father. It was a simple case of revenge.

CARL: No, Jenkins, no. Karen didn't do it. *They* did it to him. They made him play the same role night after night, year in and year out. To a true artist that deadly repetition can only lead to one of two things: alcoholism or madness. My father was a consummate artist, Jenkins . . . He resorted to both of them!

JENKINS: You mean . . .

CARL: Year in and year out, Carlton Stone played on like a shadow. He was a perfectionist.

JENKINS: Great Scott!

CARL: Yes, Jenkins. My father died to perfect the role of the ghost!

(*Blackout. End of Act II.*)

ACT III

Scene: Same as Acts I and II. ELFIE *and* CARL *are warming up for* JENKINS' *studio performance.*

CARL: There's just one thing I don't understand, Elfie. If Grotowski calls his book "Towards a Poor Theatre," why does the book cost fifteen dollars?

ELFIE: Let's exercise.

CARL: I'll watch.

ELFIE: Carl, what do you do for exercise?

CARL: I act.

ELFIE: That's not enough. If you want to be a great actor, you must hone your body. Yoga is designed to unite the body with the soul. A lot of people think that the brain is the most important organ of the body. It simply isn't true. The Japanese have a saying: "If the liver is not in good condition, neither is the disposition."

CARL: What do you think is the most important organ of the body, Elfie?

ELFIE: The heart. What do you think is the most important organ?

CARL: (*Pause*) Let's exercise.

ELFIE: Okay. Let's start with the Salute to the Sun. (CARL *gives an army salute.*) Oh, Carl, try being serious. And remember to inhale and exhale.

CARL: I will try to keep that in mind.

ELFIE: Okay, so start in a prayer position, and follow me. (*She goes through the exercise smoothly.* CARL *tries, but cannot bend to the floor.* ELFIE *continues exercising.*) Grab your ankles, put your head to your knees, with the palms of your hands to the floor . . .

CARL: Elfie, I can't get my hands to the floor.

ELFIE: Why not?

CARL: I don't know. I think my pants are too tight.

ELFIE: Continue.

(ELFIE *finishes the exercise.* CARL *continues to try to reach the floor, and by heavy breathing finally makes it. He gasps with relief.*)

CARL: I see. You breathe in. And then you breathe out.

HELGA: (*Entering with* EDMUND *and* JENKINS) . . . and when I was at the Yale Drama School, the students stood on the back of the chairs and applauded for twenty minutes. They couldn't get enough of me. (*Pause.*) They've been rehearsing for days.

EDMUND: Rehearsing?

HELGA: Yes, it's Jenkins' play—what was it called? *Dinosaur Dung,* wasn't it?

EDMUND: (*Laughing*) *Fossil Fuel,* my dear. But then you're joking, aren't you?

HELGA: (*In a loud whisper*) Don't make me laugh. It's supposed to be a tragedy.

(*They take seats in the theatre.*)

HELGA: (*Calling affectionately*) Carl! (*With difficulty.*) Son. How are you doing?

CARL: It's not how I'm doing, but what I'm doing that I keep asking myself.

HELGA: I mean the play. How is it going?

JENKINS: (*In a temper*) It's a joke! All a big joke.

HELGA: A joke?

CARL: Don't pay any attention to him. (*Aside.*) It's going brilliantly. He's nervous, that's all.

EDMUND: (*Condescending*) Opening night jitters? Stage fright? I have no sympathy for actors trembling in the wings. If you want to go on the stage, then get on with it.

HELGA: Carl, what kind of character do you play?

CARL: Well, there aren't really any characters in the play.

HELGA: No characters? Then how do you tell the story?

CARL: It doesn't have a story, either. In a way it's all the stories that ever were, rolled into one . . . and there are these images . . .

JENKINS: Carl, please, you shouldn't be out front. You should be in your place. You're spoiling the whole illusion.

CARL: Excuse me.

HELGA: (*To* CARL, *half humorously*) Break a leg! (*To* EDMUND.) Aren't they cute?

EDMUND: I hope this won't take too long.

HELGA: I think they're ready to begin.

EDMUND: I mean the performance.

JENKINS: Ladies and Gentlemen . . .

HELGA: (*To* EDMUND) Shhh, they're beginning.

GILBERT: (*Entering obtrusively in spite of himself, with script in hand*) "Pardon me for living, but" . . . (*Realizes that the performance has begun.*) Oh . . . dear me . . . I'm interrupting . . . I mean I'm late. (*Exits.*)

HELGA: (*Aside, incredulously, to* EDMUND) Did you hear what he said? "Pardon me for living!"

EDMUND: Some things are unpardonable.

JENKINS: I'll begin all over again. Where was I?

EDMUND: You were saying, "Ladies and Gentlemen."

JENKINS: Oh, yes, Ladies and Gentlemen, *Fossil Fuel* by James Jenkins. Starring . . . Elfie Fey as the Allmother and Carlton Stone, Jr. as her son.

HELGA: (*Under her breath*) There's something decadent about this.

CARL: (*From the side, imploring her*) Mother, please!

HELGA: Carl, this reminds me of the time I played Arkadina in *The Seagull*. "O Hamlet, thou has cleft my heart in twain."

CARL: "Throw away the worser part and live the better with the other half."

HELGA: Did I tell you about the time I appeared at the Yale Drama School . . .

EDMUND: (*Applauding*) Brava, Helga, Brava!

CARL: Sit down, Mother.

(*The curtain opens revealing* ELFIE *wrapped in white sheets on a phoney-looking stage rock.*)

JENKINS: The action of the play is set nine thousand nine hundred and ninety-nine years in the future after the ecological disaster. All life has been blotted out, all is empty, all is null, all is void.

HELGA: She's not wearing any makeup.

(*During the following,* JENKINS *periodically yells "Cue!" and a bell rings.* CARL *attaches strings to* ELFIE *and the set.*)

ELFIE: OOOOOOOOOOMMMMMMau! OMMMMMMMMMMMMMMMMMau! Ommmmmmmmmmmmmau! (*Screams.*) OOOOOOOOOOOMMM-MMMMMMMAU! OOOOmmmmmAAAAAuuuuu! Haya HeeYah Haya HeeeYah Hayaheeeyah. (*Grunts.*) My wooommmmbb! Nunga nunga nunga nunga nunga nunga. (*Then she breaks out of the scene and says matter-of-factly.*) Rebirth. (*She then lays on her back and enacts ritual labor pains.*) Labor Ritual/May Day—Unyin Square. (*Screams experimentally.*)

HELGA: This is either pure madness or pure genius. But I can't tell which.

GILBERT: (*Poking his head in*) There's such a thin line, I think.

HELGA: (*Whispering hoarsely to* EDMUND) Who *is* that man!

EDMUND: Why don't you ask him?

ELFIE: Mankind, man unkind, mankind, man unkind, mankind, man unkind.

HELGA: The lady doth protest too much, methinks!

ELFIE: (*Screaming in labor*) EEEEEEEEYow! EEEEEEEEYOW! EEEEEEEEYOW!

HELGA: Oh, for God's sake, is that caterwauling starting up again?

(*Smoke bombs go off.* CARL *crawls out from between* ELFIE*'s legs, and is wailing like a baby.*)

HELGA: I smell sulphur. Is that necessary.?

JENKINS: Yes, it's intentional.

HELGA; (*Laughing*) Oh, it's a stage effect! I like that.

EDMUND: It smells like the devil! If you wanted fog, why didn't you use the fog machine? At least dry ice doesn't smell.

JENKINS: I didn't want fog. I wanted smoke!

EDMUND: Well, what's the difference! (*Aside to* HELGA.) They want to work in the theatre, but they don't want to know its effects!

HELGA: The theatre is chilly tonight.

JENKINS: (*Flaring up, loudly*) That does it! The play is over! That's enough! Curtain!

CARL: But we haven't finished.

JENKINS: Enough! Curtain! (*Stamping his foot.*) Bring down the curtain! (*Finally lowers it himself.*) You must forgive me. I forgot that only the chosen few can write plays and act in them. I have infringed on a monopoly! My life . . . The theatre . . . Oh, what's the use! (*He makes a helpless gesture and exits.*)

HELGA: What's the matter with him?

CARL: You hurt his feelings.

HELGA: What did I say? The theatre *is* chilly tonight. He said himself it was going to be a joke. Now he wants to be taken seriously! I know what's behind all of this. He's trying to make us feel guilty that we're doing the classics. He's jealous of the classics. I'll bet he just wishes he could write a play as good as . . . as good as *Hamlet!* But no! He'll never admit to any feelings of inferiority. He covers up with his ravings about new forms. I think what he calls new forms are nothing but bad manners!

ELFIE: We meant to give you pleasure.

HELGA: Really? Then why don't you do the usual sort of play and not make us listen to your obscene noises?

(ELFIE *stalks off.* CARL *follows.*)

Charles Ludlam

GILBERT: (*Entering behind* HELGA *and* EDMUND, *dressed as the Ghost*) You shouldn't wound young people's pride like that.

HELGA: (*Turning*) Sir, I'll thank you to mind your own business! (*She turns back with a horror-stricken look on her face.*) OMIGOD!

EDMUND: What is it?

HELGA: It can't be . . .

EDMUND: What?

HELGA: For a moment I thought it was Carlton!

EDMUND: Calm yourself, my dear. You're imagining it.

HELGA: If you think I'm imagining it: Look!

EDMUND: (*Turns, looks at* GILBERT, *and screams*) Give me some light!

(*There is a blackout. Applause. Lights come up on* HELGA *and* EDMUND *in their* Hamlet *costumes, bowing. They try to steal an extra bow, but the applause dies suddenly, stopping them in their tracks. Flustered, they exit into the dressing room.*)

HELGA: Did you know about this meeting?

EDMUND: Carl told Jenkins to pass it around.

HELGA: What do you expect?

EDMUND: Either a pathetic abdication speech or a power grab. I'm ready for either.

HELGA: Is our protégé, Elfie Fey, going to be at this meeting?

JENKINS: No, she's not.

HELGA: Oh, she didn't take her call.

CARL: (*Entering*) Mother. Mr. Dundreary. Where's Jenkins?

JENKINS: Here I am.

CARL: Is Elfie here?

JENKINS: (*Darkly*) No Carl, she's not. She said she was going down to the river.

CARL: Omigod!

EDMUND: Now, Carl, I know you murdered Gilbert Fey.

CARL: It was an accident. It wasn't a real rapier. The blade retracts into the handle—like you said.

EDMUND: Who would believe it? He had just told you that he killed your father.

CARL: How did you know that?

EDMUND: (*Pointing to the keyhole*) The keyhole.

CARL: This is blackmail.

EDMUND: That's one word for it. I call it the simple economics of discretion.

CARL: What do you want?

EDMUND: Your company, your role, your mother, and your name.

CARL: My name?

EDMUND: Yes, the name Stone is a theatrical trademark. (*Brandishing a contract.*) And you're going to sell it to me for the legal sum of $1.00—and agree to act only in London.

CARL: Why in London?

EDMUND: Twill not be noticed there. The acting there is as bad as yours. Sign on the dotted line.

JENKINS: Don't sign. Carl. Don't give anything to that sleazy son of a bitch.

EDMUND: Sign, or I'll blab to the police.

CARL: They have me where they want me. (*Signs.*) Uncle Gilbert didn't do it. Are you people blind? Can't you see that he was shielding someone? It was Elfie—Elfie killed my father!

HELGA: What was her motive?

CARL: He tried to drown her when she was a little child, left her to be raised by the petty bourgeoisie. Then, as her artistic aspirations grew and were thwarted, so did her resentment, and now . . . now she's gone down to the river!

ELFIE: (*Entering in a wet swimsuit*) Of course I went down to the river. I always take a swim after a performance.

JENKINS: Elfie didn't do it, Carl. It was Edmund and your mother. They are . . . they have been . . .

HELGA: There's no need for delicacy, Jenkins. You're trying to say that Edmund and I had a "special relationship." Well, it's true and Carl knows all about it.

JENKINS: Then you admit it?

HELGA: I admit to having a lover, but not to being a murderess. I told you, Carl, it was suicide.

CARL: Pop was discovered poisoned by the dread hebenon poured into the porches of his ear. I think that's a rather unlikely way to commit suicide.

EDMUND: Really, people wouldn't believe this if it were acted upon the stage!

CARL: Someone in this company killed my father (*to the audience*) and we're not leaving this theatre until we find out who it is. Each of you had a motive. If only one of you didn't, then we could suspect the least likely person.

ELFIE: You're just like Hamlet, seeking to avenge your father's death.

CARL: That would be neat, Elfie. But it wouldn't quite be true. How can I seek revenge for something I have done myself so often in my dreams? I know I should be horrified by all this. I know I should seek the murderer out of moral indignation or revenge. But the truth is that the situation in the abstract has so taken hold of me that I have come to regard the actors in it as merely pieces in a puzzle, baffling and fascinating to the point of monomania.

GILBERT: (*Entering*) So you thought you could get away from me, did you, you little slut! You're coming home with me!

CARL: Uncle Gilbert!

GILBERT: You swore to me!

CARL: And I swear now.

ELFIE: There's no need to swear, Carl. (*To* GILBERT.) I heard everything, Uncle Gilbert. Did you think that anything could keep me away from the theatre? I would defy you forever. (*To* CARL.) Carl, I'm convinced of your greatness as an actor now. You were able to convince me that you didn't love me.

CARL: But Elfie, Carlton was my father, too . . . That makes you my sister.

HELGA: That's where you're wrong, son. Your father was no actor. You were the son of a plumber. That accounts for your knack in fixing the W.C., and why you're not blond.

CARL: (*To* ELFIE) Now there's nothing standing in our way . . . Tell me, all of you, who was the greatest actor that ever lived?

EDMUND: Sir Johnston Forbes Robertson.

HELGA: Modjeska.

ELFIE: Eleonora Duse.

JENKINS: Chaucey Allcott.

CARL: Henry Irving.

GILBERT: The greatest actor who ever lived was Carlton Stone, Sr.!

CARL: You say that, Uncle Gilbert? After all he put you through? Really, I think you're being more than generous. Oh, Pop was a great personality, it's true, but an actor in the true sense? Not really. Why, Pop never heard of Grotowski! He never did his yoga. Why, his idea of a great play was a play with a good part in it for him! A great speech was a speech he could give with bombast. No, I think Pop was little more than a ham.

GILBERT: Carl, how could you?

CARL: (*Shamed*) Perhaps I'm being a little harsh on Pop. He did have perfect timing. Why, even his death was so perfectly timed that it revealed his friend's secret ambition, his wife's adultery, and loyalty in a man he thought was his enemy. In all of his career, Pop only stepped out of character once: when he took exception to his son's assertion that Irving was anything to compare with his old man!! (*Removes* GILBERT's *disguise, revealing him to be* CARLTON.)

ALL: Carlton!

STONE: Carl, when did you guess?

CARL: Well, Pop, you didn't give yourself away until the play within the play scene. I saw you come on as the Ghost, and I remembered something you said, "In order to play Carlton, you have to have been Carlton" . . . There's just one thing I can't figure out, Pop, who is Elfie Fey?

STONE: My mistress, young man, my mistress.

HELGA: Well!

ELFIE: I'm sorry, Carl. You're just too immature for me.

STONE: Sorry to cut you out of the action, son.

CARL: That's alright, you two. I'm having a rather interesting "experimental" relationship: with Jenkins!

HELGA: It's a mother's dream come true. To have a son who's gay!

EDMUND: Helga, you told me you did it.

HELGA: I wanted to do something to make you admire me.

EDMUND: A remark like that could cost me my job.

STONE: Edmund, you're a scoundrel. But I like a good scoundrel, so I'm giving you a raise. That's not bad coming from a man who knows you're fucking his wife, is it?

EDMUND: (*Beaming*) You're one in a million.

CARL: That's my Pop!

HELGA: (*Indignant*) Yesterday I felt positively wanton. Now I'm beginning to feel a little hemmed in.

STONE: By the way, Edmund, I hear you bought my name. That name was, in fact, Raymond Fey. And that's the name you're going to be acting under from now on: Ray Fey! Here's your itching powder, Ray; (*opens paper and blows powder on* EDMUND) and all along I thought I had crabs. (*To* CARL.) You see, my boy, all this was contrived . . .

CARL: It certainly was.

STONE: . . .to teach you a little lesson.

EDMUND: Don't make hangmen of your superiors.

HELGA: That although there is only one way of being born, there are many ways of getting killed.

JENKINS: Never suspend your disbelief.

ELFIE: And that the important thing in life is not to tell the truth, but to perfect the mask!

STONE: Ah, yes, we all learned something along the way. But I just wanted to teach you that in order to play Hamlet, you have to have been Hamlet. And from what I see in these reviews, you *were* Hamlet out there tonight.

ALL: Reviews!!!!

(STONE *hands out newspapers to all present.*)

EDMUND: "The costumes were beautiful." *Women's Wear Daily.*

HELGA: "An unmasculine Hamlet." *New York Post.*

ELFIE: "Exhilarating." *New York Times.*

JENKINS: "Stones Hone Bard's Bones." *Variety.*

ELFIE: A *Hamlet* with a happy ending!

HELGA: Very hedonistic!

EDMUND: (*In the voice of Eric Blore*) Very eighteenth century!

JENKINS: And very advanced dramaturgically.

CARL: Gee, Dad, the rest is silence?

STONE: Is there any music to compare with it? (*Hands recorder to* CARL *who miraculously beings to play* "Greensleeves.")

(STONE *and* ELFIE *exit, while* CARL *plays the recorder.*)

CARL: (*Suddenly very excited*) Jenkins, I'm going to do your play!

JENKINS: *Fossil Fuel?*

CARL: Well, that's the only play you've written, isn't it?

JENKINS: Yes.

CARL: Until we do that one, you'll never get on to the next.

JENKINS: Oh, no!

CARL: What is it now, Jenkins?

JENKINS: If people are beginning to like my work, there must be something wrong with it.

EDMUND: (*Shocked*) Jenkins, you're a snob. And here all along I thought you were a communist. (*Gives* HELGA *a jewel case which she opens; a mouse pops out. They exit laughing.*)

CARL: Jim, there's just one thing I can't figure out. Pop was playing dead in the dressing room, but we saw him go on as the Ghost. How could he be in two places at the same time!

JENKINS: Beats me.

STONE: (*Reentering*) Jenkins, are you going hunting tomorrow?

JENKINS: Hunting?!

STONE: For props.

JENKINS: Yes.

STONE: I've just remembered. We've run out of stage blood.

(*Enter the Ghost, reading* Variety.)

END

Kenneth Bernard & John Vaccaro
A Collaboration

gerald rabkin

Since 1968, John Vaccaro has staged six of Kenneth Bernard's plays: two short plays—*The Lovers* and *The Monkeys of the Organ Grinder*— at the New Theatre Workshop, and four major plays—*The Moke-Eater, Night Club, The Magic Show of Dr. Ma-Gico,* and *The Sixty-Minute Queer Show*—under the banner of The Play-House of the Ridiculous. Vaccaro was forced by illness to relinquish directing yet another, *King Humpy.* This fruitful collaboration has revealed the dark side of the Ridiculous comic vision. In contrast to Tavel's arch verbalism and Ludlam's distinctive blend of travesty and tradition, Bernard brought to the Ridiculous a nightmare imagination rooted in the grotesque. He did not reject the playfulness, the phallicism, the sexual ambiguity that had characterized early Ridiculous work. But he subordinated them and added a scream of pain.

Bernard has been able to work successfully with a directorial auteur of strong theatrical will because of his own fascination with the metaphor of theatricality. His major plays are all structured on, or incorporate, the idea of the "show," with its segmented "acts" as opposed to conventional dramatic narrative. *The Sixty-Minute Queer Show* (1977) moves back an additional step to include the process of theatrical creation. In the play Bernard incorporates scenes of the Play-

Originally published in *Performing Arts Journal* 3, no. 1 (spring /summer 1978). Reprinted with permission.

House of the Ridiculous in rehearsal. The "Director" is a thinly veiled portrait of Vaccaro at work—not a naturalistic portrait, but one nevertheless instantly recognizable.

The rehearsal-in-a-play device is, of course, familiar to all viewers or readers of Pirandello and his followers. Bernard honors this tradition by consciously obliterating the boundary between artifice and reality; the manic farce in *The Queer Show* turns disturbingly real. On another level, Bernard uses the conceit, as he does various theatrical elements, as a means of aesthetic disorientation, a framing device that forces upon the viewer a disequilibrium of expectation. By incorporating into his play not a caricature of a director, but an essentially accurate portrait of Vaccaro at work, played by himself, Bernard acknowledges the creative individuality of his major theatrical collaborator. The Director in *The Queer Show* plays much the same role that Masters of Ceremonies (in more ways than one) play in Bernard's other works. Alec in *The Moke-Eater,* Bubi in *Night Club,* and Dr. Ma-Gico in *The Magic Show of Dr. Ma-Gico* are all "directors" of the various turns and vignettes that comprise the "shows" they present. On one level, Bernard's major plays are dissections of theatrical process and directorial power.

Since the image of the director as tyrant-savior is central to Bernard's vision, it inevitably demands a real director of strength and authority to realize it. But is Vaccaro the director to realize faithfully *any* playwright's vision? He has had the reputation of imposing upon indifferent or terrible plays his idiosyncratic personal style. Some have maintained that his aesthetic is "the worse script the better." By cajoling, prodding, and sadistically whipping his minions into a frenzy, so received opinion goes, Vaccaro has created a theatre in which visual and aural imagery triumphs over language and meaning.

It is about time this assessment was laid to rest. By his own admission, Vaccaro is "not one of those people who can work without words." He has *never* worked, à la Chaikin, Grotowski, the Becks, without a play as foundation. In many respects he is a "classical," traditional director. Improvisation in his theatre is always rooted in the specific dramatic context of a given play. The overdramatized, seeming non-acting of his performers derives not from Schechnerian self-examination, but from the self-conscious parodic style demanded by the first playwright of the Ridiculous, Ronald Tavel, and by Vaccaro's search for the means to express it. The extremities of Ridiculous performance flow from the requirements of its "operatic" style, and from Vaccaro's insistence that his performers hold nothing back; they must go all the way, release everything buried in the character or situation they are enacting.

Vaccaro's directional "sadism" is itself a role, one which his actors—many of whom have worked with him through the years—accept as such. It mirrors the abandon he demands of them. If they must release all, so must he. The cardinal principle of Vaccaro and his Play-House is that you can make no demands on the audience you do not first make on yourself. Hence Vaccaro's "demonic" directorial style: his irony, ridicule, and egocentric relentlessness. In a sense, no less than his fellow standard-bearer of the Ridiculous, Charles Ludlam, Vaccaro is his own star performer, although he has appeared irregularly throughout the years in various Play-House productions. By incorporating the persona of Vaccaro into *The Sixty-Minute Queer Show,* Bernard has not invented a role; he has absorbed one.

It is true that when faced with a weak script Vaccaro has proven himself a master of theatrical camouflage, of presenting a dizzying whirl of visual imagery and music designed to transcend textual deficiencies. But he has never deliberately sought out weak plays; it is just that good ones which match his theatrical vision are hard to find. The reputation for textual butchery derives from Vaccaro's hatred of verbosity. His theatrical means demand a script that is brief, intense, concentrated. If he proceeds with an overwritten text, he will cut it unmercifully. The early collaboration with Ron Tavel foundered primarily because Tavel's Ridiculous style increasingly found expression in multifaceted effusions of language. To Vaccaro, Tavel's plays became wordy; to Tavel, free linguistic experiment was essential to his work. A break was inevitable.

In Bernard, on the other hand, Vaccaro found a playwright whose dramatic style, as well as thematic concerns, matched his own.

Bernard's plays, on all counts, affirm Vaccaro's theatrical values: they are brief (an hour to an hour and a half), concise, intense, disorienting, outrageous, and fiercely ironic. With such plays as dramatic foundation, Vaccaro has not felt the necessity of radical surgery. According to Bernard, up until *The Queer Show* his plays have been mounted with fidelity—a fact confirmed by comparing Vaccaro's productions with Bernard's original texts.

It was a fortuitous meeting: Vaccaro found in Bernard's plays the perfect dramatic vehicle for the manic style he had evolved. And the play's helped refine that style, for Bernard's dramatic vision was much bleaker than Tavel's, much more concerned with the dark forces that govern human experience. By confronting Bernard's plays, the Play-House deepened its concerns and invested its pop art imagery with more disturbing resonances.

And Bernard found in Vaccaro and his Play-House a theatre not confined by the cautions of theatrical conventionality, a theatre "willing to abandon the traditional modes of vocal and physical stage expression and the traditional mode of what is proper ideologically and structurally to a play." Bernard's plays demand a constant level of intensity and energy the Play-House has been able to provide without compromise. His plays indeed abound in "bad taste" and "cruelty," for he is merciless in his dissection of the lies, deceits, atrocities, and betrayals that comprise human reality.

Is their work, as some claim, nihilistic and despairing? The best reply is a note Bernard appended to the program of the Atlanta production of *Night Club:* "If there is any hope at all for mankind, it lies in honesty and recognition of reality, particularly the unreconstructed and unreconstructible nature of the human creature. Man, I would hope, endures *in spite of.* His dignity, courage, and beauty do (sometimes) triumph sufficiently over the grossness of finitude to lift our spirits. It is my wish that plays like *Night Club* encourage, even demand, such honesty and recognition, even while they 'entertain' (and I do insist on that)."

● ● ●

The collaboration between Bernard and Vaccaro began with *The Moke-Eater* in 1968. Although the late sixties was a time of diverse theatrical experimentation, Bernard didn't like much of what he saw. One of the few pieces he did like was the "Motel" sequence from *America Hurrah*, with its huge, destructive puppets. In 1967, Bernard was taken by a friend to the Bouwerie Lane Theatre where a group called The Play-House of the Ridiculous was presenting a science-fiction travesty called *The Conquest of the Universe* by Charles Ludlam. Although he couldn't understand much of the dialogue, Bernard was impressed by the piece's energy and atmosphere, its sense of total theatre.

He sent a note to the director and asked if he read outside scripts. Vaccaro responded positively and Bernard sent him copies of three plays, one of which was *The Moke-Eater*. What Bernard didn't know was that at the time Vaccaro received the plays he had considered abandoning directing. The Play-House was undergoing an internal crisis that resulted in the defection of several performers, including Charles Ludlam, who had set up his own company to present another version of his play. The crisis atmosphere had thoroughly demoralized Vaccaro, but after he read *The Moke-Eater*, his creative energy was reawakened. It represented a marked departure from the customary Ridiculous style evolved during the Tavel collaborations. It had a linear narrative about a salesman who finds himself stranded among a group of hostile villagers and is increasingly tormented by them. But the style was far from naturalistic, the energy of the piece was unrelenting, and the bleak vision of American society presented conformed completely to Vaccaro's own.

Remember the political turmoil of the late sixties; although the Play-House has never been a political theatre in a narrow sense, from its very inception in the mid-sixties it severely repudiated American middle-class values. Its obscenity and playful phallicism—which seem so tame in this Age of Pornography—embroiled it in constant conflict with the forces of Puritanical repression. Its theatrical tenets—the celebration of bad taste, the obliteration of rigid gender roles, its anti-heroic irreverence—ridiculed the most cherished pieties of bourgeois America. Although it abhorred political rhetoric and naive romanticism, the Play-House was essentially an anarchistic theatre.

The Moke-Eater, it seemed to Vaccaro, spoke to the urgencies of the time and demanded production. It merged in his head with the aural image of people slobbering over their food in the 14th Street Automat. He decided to direct it, and after a summer of work, it opened in September 1968 at Max's Kansas City. The production subsequently moved to the Cafe Au Go-Go, and was revived in the spring of 1969 at the Gotham Art Theatre on West 43rd Street.

The play is a fierce, violent nightmare vision of America, an assault on innocence that can recognize neither the evil it confronts nor the evil it creates. A traveling salesman, Jack, finds himself stranded in a prototypical American small town when his car breaks down. Instead of concerned good will, he is met by sinister, animalistic anticipation. The townspeople welcome him gleefully as someone desperately awaited named Fred, a designation Jack vehemently rejects. The townspeople, unhappy that he is unwilling to admit that he is Fred, turn dark and threatening, and led by their grimly ironic Boss, Alec, submit the hapless Jack to a series of grotesque humiliations that leave him physically and psychically stripped.

With Alec as Master of Ceremonies, Jack is forced to witness or participate in a sadistic series of charades—such as having to play Amos and Andy in hastily applied blackface—which he has no choice but to endure. Finally, reduced to impotent infantilism, he will admit anything, even that he is Fred, and is allowed to leave town; but not before he observes the Moke-Eater—the amorphous manifestation of the destructive energy of the play—devour an old man as victim. But the escape is itself a charade. "The little show" is not over: as Jack's repaired car speeds quickly away, the townspeople freeze in the precise positions they held at the beginning of the play. The door opens and Jack reenters; his car has broken down again. Although he left three hours ago, he has not left, he cannot leave, he will never leave.

In production, Vaccaro made Jack's fate explicit by having the townspeople eviscerate him (hands twisting entrails were projected on his stomach) in the exact manner horribly described by Alec earlier in the play. The explicitness underlined a production that was pitiless both to the audience and particularly to the actor playing Jack. Vaccaro infused his performers with a demonic energy that was deliberately provocative. He had them study the paintings of Hieronymous Bosch for visual inspiration. As the play progressed they donned feathers and furs, becoming part animal, part bird, less human. They collectively offered an image of implacable, terrifying irrationality.

The Moke-Eater directed itself primarily to the falseness of American values: to the myth of Our Town hospitality, to the refusal of the naive American to accept the reality of evil, the dark forces, the "Fred" within himself—a refusal that is fatal. In Vaccaro and Bernard's next major collaboration the theme was more ambitious: not only the Death of America, but the Death of Civilization itself.

Night Club, which opened in September 1970 at La Mama E.T.C., may well be Bernard's finest achievement. It takes place in the moment before Apocalypse. In Bubi's Hide-Away, a small, subterranean, windowless room, an androgynous compère presides over a show comprised of a series of inept, desperate acts performed by members of the audience themselves: a ventriloquist unable to control his lecherous, foul-mouthed female dummy, a juggler who destroys expensive crockery and antiques, a loquacious Greek who offers vile impersonations of a southern belle and a Nazi sadist, and "The Grand Kabuki Theatre of America," which absurdly translates a banal campus romance into the guttural sonorities of the classical Japanese tradition.

The spirit of the proceedings is far removed from the one-joke comic ineptitudes of *El Grande de Coca-Cola*. Bubi effusively presides over the mangled performances with all the hyperbolic enthusiasm he can muster. He throws kisses, bumps and grinds, camps, cajoles, insults—*anything* to keep the show going. The audience onstage—clearly a surrogate for the actual audience—responds with desperation and dependency, anxiety and fear. They intone Bubi's name as though it were a major charm in a manner sexual, ritualistic, and incantatory. Only he can save them, only he can hold back the moment of truth when the darkness outside the Hide-Away will break in and envelop them.

Does anything exist outside the room? Sounds of marching, explosions, jackhammers seep through the walls of the refuge. The Hide-

Away is cramped, rotten, decaying, but it is all that remains: the Last Bunker. Bubi drops his cheerful hysteria from time to time and desperately tries to communicate with someone—anyone—outside: "Hello, out there. Hello, out there. This is Bubi calling again, Bubi from Bubi's Hide-Away. . . . Our walls are crumbling, we have no resistance. We have no place to go. We cannot come out. . . . We are flesh, we are naked, we are helpless. . . . We are gathered here, in this hole, our last retreat, to give succor and solace to each other. . . . Do you hear me? . . . Answer, respond, acknowledge, communicate, relieve us, for we cannot last, we . . . cannot . . . *last.*"

There is no reply. All Bubi can do is to escalate the desperate diversions. Finally, the show reaches a literal climax as Bubi encourages the audience to join in a mass copulation accompanied by the Lone Ranger theme from *Wilhelm Tell.* Sex is the ultimate anodyne. One young man refuses to join in, even after his girlfriend has disappeared in the communal embrace. "The menu says there is no cover charge!" he insists. But Bubi wryly points out, "There's always a cover charge, darling, didn't you know?" and the young man is dragged screaming to the stage and beheaded on a makeshift guillotine. And as Bubi, with profound love and sincerity, cajoles new "tricks, songs, dances" from his desperate charges, even the severed head of the young man responds with reciprocal ardor: "Bubi! Bubi! Bubi!"

Vaccaro's production hewed closely to the line of Bernard's terrifying image of cosmic indifference. Apart from cutting one number—a ferociously ironic send-up of racism that used gross black stereotypes—because he feared the irony would be misunderstood (remember the racial climate of 1970), Vaccaro had the innovative idea of magnifying the dominance of the androgynous Bubi by having him/her played by *two* performers—male and female, identically garbed—with one repeating the other's lines as a kind of mike echo.

Where do you go after you've destroyed civilization? Bubi offered, if not a solution, a suggestion: you concentrate on diversionary tactics to distract the executioner; you stretch your comic routine at the gallows as long as permitted. *The Magic Show of Dr. Ma-Gico,* as Bernard and Vaccaro's next offering, which opened at La Mama in March 1973, did not differ from Bubi's Revue in its essential theme: the holding power of art—even inept art if need be—against the gathering apocalypse. In *Night Club,* apart from the Kabuki sequence, the aesthetic materials were contemporary. In *Dr. Ma-Gico,* Bernard broadened his metaphor to confront the ambiguities of the cultural tradition: its enduring beauty and its irrelevance.

He started with the dreadful paradox recorded in George Steiner's *Language and Silence:* that SS men returned from a day at the gas chambers and crematoria to glory in the beauties of Bach and Mozart. What is the value of culture, both Steiner and Bernard ask, if it doesn't prevent you from killing people? Steiner wonders if the only appropriate artistic response is silence. Bernard, recognizing that the question is unanswerable, goes the opposite route: he screams.

Dr. Ma-Gico is set in the past, in a court suggestive of that of Louis XIV. Bernard's materials are courtly, romantic, fairy tale—but his use of them is anything but gentle and nostalgic. The magician, Dr. Ma-Gico, for the "entertainment" of his entourage, conjures up a series of episodes that uniformly end in betrayal and/or horror: a Duke convinces the King that a young student has won his daughter's love through deceit. Without allowing the young man a defense, the King has him hanged. The body—which achieves erection in death—is granted to a lecherous, ugly, old widow as reward for her husband's services. The young man unexpectedly revives. The Duke insists he be hanged again, but the crone claims her prize. The young man has no choice but to submit to her scabrous embrace. "And so," Dr. Ma-Gico benignly summarizes, "justice again triumphs . . . and the good people of my court are entertained for a day. God is truly bountiful."

Justice "triumphs" similarly in later episodes that escalate in violence and cruelty: Esmeralda is torn to pieces by gypsies who demand she dance for them; a younger lover, to prove his fidelity, accepts the lecherous embraces of another diseased old crone and is castrated by her during fellatio; a Prince has to decide whether a fat, ugly dancer or an old, slobbering King is his enchanted Princess, and makes a fatal mistake; a Queen is fucked to death by her royal consort; and, finally, Ma-Gico slits the throat of a suspicious King.

Kenneth Bernard and John Vaccaro

A grim catalogue; Bernard uses the images and conventions of folktales and romance to cumulatively indict the mendacities of human beings, particularly those *in power*. He is fascinated by the image of the King, the ultimate symbol of authority. It is not an unambiguous image: on one level, the images of political and artistic power are opposed; but on another, the illusionist-artist plays the King as well as his assassin. Bernard implies that art itself has its dangerous, demonic, and corrupt components.

A cold play—severe, remote, with much less humor than is characteristic of the Bernard–Vaccaro collaborations. The horrors of the episodes are framed and distanced by stylized sequences of courtly gavottes and minuets danced by Ma-Gico's entourage, sequences that cut the horrific episodes like the silent slice of a guillotine blade. As always, Bernard seeks to shock the audience into seeing itself in the grotesque charades enacted before it. For this reason he specifies in his text that in addition to the central image of the throne, the set include a row of mirrors encircling the stage. From these vivid images, Vaccaro constructed a distorted vision of baroque courtliness. On a diamond chessboard floor surrounded by mylar mirrors, the actors whirled frenetically like music box puppets. The production was a scrupulous and faithful realization of Bernard's play.

The image of the King continues to fascinate Bernard. It is central to every episode in another collaboration with The Play-House of the Ridiculous, *The Sixty-Minute Queer Show*. The play carries forward *Ma-Gico's* preoccupation with the violence of authority. In the "Cottage Banquet" sequence, the lecherous King uses his power to food-rape a shepherdess; in the "Court Games" sequence the scene is continued: the king is put on trial for his abuse of power. He is stripped of his finery but insists on wearing his crown: "*I* am justice. . . . Power always wears a crown!" The shepherd presents the indictment: how he and his daughter were happy in their simple pleasures until the King came, engorged his daughter with food, and "killed" the slender reed she had been by transforming her into a mountain of fat. The executioner—as actor—asks for the verdict: "*Line*, please!" His knife is poised at the King's throat as the scene ends. The climax of the King's appearance is his assassination—as in *Ma-Gico*—in the play's final sequence. He bleeds to death in a pool of spurting blood as a drag queen presents a manic, camp monologue of loss: "I have never felt so *stranded* in my life."

The dual images of drag queen and threatened King poetically unify what seems on the surface to be a formless piece. Bernard's method in *The Queer Show* is more oblique than in his other Play-House collaborations. There is no through narrative as in *The Moke-Eater*, no dominant figure like Bubi or Ma-Gico to order the proceedings, although the Director partially fulfills this role. What we have is a show that offers monologues, turns, sequences which sustain a vaudevillesque metaphor but which seem unrelated. The materials of these sequences derive from both the past and present: a conflation of the metaphors of *Night Club* and *Dr. Ma-Gico:* court games, Turkish boudoir, circus, hillbilly farmhouse, interspersed with comic, desperate monologues and assorted turns by a series of drag queens.

But *The Queer Show* is less chaotic than at first meets the eye or ear. As always, Bernard and Vaccaro are concerned less with "rational," linear theatre than with a theatre of images that resonate beyond conscious understanding. Bernard has asserted that "the process of rationalization is a mistake," that the best of plays, even naturalistic ones, work best on the level of metaphor. The senses, not the intellect, must be engaged to evoke the power of dream, myth, fairy tale. "I try to fill the void of plot with some existing and recognizable ritual."

The Queer Show presents through the frenetic style of the Ridiculous a consciously incongruous, disoriented, bizarre vision of reality. Because according to Bernard and Vaccaro that is the only way reality can be truthfully portrayed. Alec, Bubi, Ma-Gico, the Director can *try* to impose an aesthetic order on meaningless flux, but their power—the artist's power—is severely limited; reality *will* break through. The King represents the order imposed from above: arbitrary, brutal, tyrannical, respectable, logical. The opposing image is that of the Queer, in the broadest meaning of the word. The opposition, however, is not simplistic: evil despot versus noble downtrodden (the oppressed can be as ugly as the King), but a dialectic of images.

Kenneth Bernard and John Vaccaro   157

The image of the Queer is crucial not only to this play but to all Bernard–Vaccaro work—indeed, to all The Play-House of the Ridiculous's work. It is frequently misunderstood because it is equated with its narrow homosexual definition. Vaccaro's theatre has been called by some "homosexual" and "woman-hating." These designations are myopic. The homosexual variation of queerness is indeed part of Vaccaro's theatre. It would be foolish to deny the centrality of homosexual sensibility: the outsider's oblique view of conventional sexuality. But Vaccaro has always rejected the idea of a coterie theatre dominated by a singular sexual orientation. His cross-sexual casting represents far more than camp self-indulgence. Particularly in his productions of Bernard's plays, which whatever their subject display no homosexual stamp whatever, *all* rigidly conventional sexual stereotypes are demolished. And far from denigrating women, the strongest roles in the collaborations have usually been played by them.

The Queer Show program listed nine different definitions of the word "queer." Queerness challenges not only the fixity of sexual roles but all the King represents: logic, order, narration, respectability, authority. In the play's farm sequence, the swishy son opposes his parents' assumption of what he is and *should be;* in the Turkish boudoir, arch-macho Don Juan is transformed into the reverse of his masculine stereotype. And nothing is queerer than sex itself; Vaccaro/Bernard accord it no solemnity. Despite the overtness of its sexual imagery the Play-House has consistently been the antithesis of a pornographic theatre. It has always exposed both the ridiculousness of sex as well as its role in the expression or repression of political power—perhaps in this age of the Joy of Sex its most radical attitude. *The Queer Show's* final image of flaming faggotry is consciously contrasted with the image of the dying King: the wish-fulfillment of the artist-magician. What is queerer? Campy extravagance which betrays real loss, or the violence and death at the heart of individuals and institutions? As the Culture Queen states, "Queer is queerer than you think."

Bernard's original text of *The Queer Show* introduced each scenic "turn" with the framing device of a monologue, mime, or dance by a drag queen; originally, there were nine such links involving ten different drag queens in varying tones and postures of hysteria, pretension, and vituperation. In directing the play—which opened in June 1977 at La Mama—Vaccaro, together with most of his performers, felt that the drag queen device was both repetitive and anachronistic, and that two of the monologues were so vituperative as to be alienating and obtrusive. He cut them and other framing devices and altered the drag queen identity of the opening monologue. Bernard felt that the central image of the play had been blurred, that the Play-House had lost its nerve, with Vaccaro and his associates uncharacteristically concerned with being liked by the audience. For the first time since the collaboration began, Bernard felt that the play he had written hadn't been given a chance. Vaccaro, in turn, felt that he was being true to the play in his customary way by making it work as effectively as possible with the performers available, that excessive aggression was counterproductive theatrically, and that Bernard had not made the seriousness of his objections as clear as he should have.

Postscript: The Bernard–Vaccaro collaboration ended in 1984, with *La Fin du Cirque* and *Play with an Ending.* Despite intimations of renewal, their artistic relationship has not resumed.

The Magic Show of Dr. Ma-Gico

kenneth bernard

The Magic Show of Dr. Ma-Gico was first performed on March 15, 1973, at La Mama E.T.C., New York. A Play-House of the Ridiculous production, it was directed by John Vaccaro. The cast included:

DR. MA-GICO   Sierra Bandit

ESMERALDA   Golda Rush

QUASIMODA   Michael Arian

Gentlemen and Ladies of the Court:

KING   Gordon Comte de Bressac

QUEEN; OLD LADY   Elsene Sorrentino

DUKE   Bela de Boite

DUCHESS; PRINCE   Estelle Bayuda

JACQUES; COURTIER   Jean d'Albano

MARQUISE   Marcia d'Imes

MARQUIS   Gare de la Pissoir

MARIE   Mallory Jones

Servants:

M. ROULADE; OLD KING   Spots Bradigan

ASSASSIN; KNAVE   Howard Solomon

WIDOW FIQUIS   Agosto Machado

DUKE'S DAUGHTER   Delia de la Bouche

VALET   Petit Boite

FAIRY PRINCESS   Belle Pavlov

CHAMBERMAID   Darlene Miller

LADY ELEANOR   Sweet Wm. Edgar

Set: Elwin Charles Terrel II
Costumes: Bernard Roth
Lighting: David Abrams
Music: Richard Weinstock
Choreography: Carolyn Lord

Fanfare. Lights. DR. MA-GICO *and his entourage are frozen onstage in dance positions. The stage is a seventeenth-century drawing room. Upstage center is a throne on a platform, behind which is a row of mirrors.* MA-GICO *is dressed in black, wears a cape and a top hat; his couture is early modern. His entourage are dressed as ladies and gentlemen of the court. Servants, jesters, etc.; dogs, birds in cages, plants. The audience sits in chairs on three sides, the first row left vacant for the gentlemen and ladies of the court. Retainers, etc., scattered about perimeters, around throne, on floor.*

MA-GICO: Ladies and gentlemen, this show begins and ends with a dance.

(*Music. A minuet. They dance, after which they clap genteelly and take their seats.*)

Ladies and gentlemen, my assistants. Esmeralda! (*Fanfare, deep curtsy.*) Quasimoda! (*Fanfare, awkward bow.*) The gentlemen and ladies of the court! (*They turn in their seats and smile at the audience.*) And (*waving his hand loosely*) . . . sundry others. (*The servants, etc., grin and wave.*) They . . . *change* from time to time. (*Polite laughter*) We bring you tonight . . . *The Magic Show!* (*Fanfare.*) Starring myself (*fanfare*), Dr. Ma-Gico, master magician! (*Fanfare; he bows.*) The first thing we do is dispense with preliminaries and expectations.

(*In quick order, with fanfares, he pulls a dead pigeon, rabbit, whatever, out of* ESMERALDA, *flicks a deck of cards over the audience, takes colored streamers out of* QUASIMODA'*s mouth, and saws a girl in a box in half as she giggles. There is never any pretense of skill, illusion, or expertise in these tricks, which he continues, at odd moments and indifferently, throughout the play. For example, the legs stick-*

ing out from the box are patently false, or they may be a man's or reversed.)

Last but not least (*he puts his hand in* ESMERALDA's *crotch*), the Fountain of Youth! (*Water spray from* ESMERALDA's *mouth. Fanfare. Bows. Polite applause.*) So much for all that. And now we dance again, but only briefly this time.

(*A few turns more of the minuet, which* MA-GICO *stops by clapping his hands when ready.*)

All right, all right. Sufficient. Sufficient. Everybody seated. Take your seats, please. *Quickly.*

(*He clears his throat, signals to the musicians. Fanfare.*)

Ladies and gentlemen, we come now to the first sequence. Or episode. There will be several of these, and you must look for a theme, continuity. But not too hard or you might miss it entirely. For example, we have a lot of kings. Perhaps you should make something of that. There's our first one over there. He is seated on his throne. In his hands he holds the symbols of his power (*a glass sphere and a scepter*). His robe is very long, longer than he is. His crown rests precariously on his head. Several feet in front of him, on the ground, is a book which he must pick up. What is in it we do not know, only that it is important and he must pick it up. Here is his problem. He must rise, and as he rises transfer both symbols of his power to one arm, so that with the other he may sweep up his robe, step forward, and, without stopping, bend and pick up the book. He must do this in a continuous, graceful, kinglike motion, without losing his crown, tripping, or dropping anything. He must not make the transfer *before* he begins to rise, nor must he arrange his robe. It is all one fluid movement, unbroken by hesitation, clumsiness, or thought. We shall give him six, eight, ten tries, perhaps more. Or less. But if he does not finally succeed, he shall die, for he is no king.—Are you ready, King?

(*The* KING *nods. The court watches intensely as he makes his attempts, emitting sighs, groans, etc.* MA-GICO *interpolates. The* KING *may succeed, but most likely not, for his task is difficult. He concentrates, sweats, becomes exhausted with anxiety and fear as his failures mount.*)

No, no, you fool! Gracefully! . . . The robe, the robe! You've stepped on it! . . . Pick it up, pick it up! No, don't fumble it! It's not a towel! . . . No, don't stop! Keep moving! Gracefully! . . . Like a king, like a king! . . . No, not yet. You can try again! . . . Now! Go on! Don't think! Move! . . .

(*The pressure builds. The task must be done perfectly. Any hesitation or clumsiness whatsoever is picked up by* MA-GICO *or the court.* MA-GICO *keeps it going as long as there is tension. When he thinks it is enough, or when he sees that the* KING's *spirit is broken, that he has given up, that he will never do it, he signals. An assassin steps forward as the* KING *stands trapped and trembling with his robe and symbols, a shambles of kingliness, and sticks a knife in his belly.*)

The king is dead!

(*Or, on those rare occasions when he might succeed.*)

Bravo. Long live the king!

(*In either case, genteel applause. Music. A lively gavotte, etc.*)

For the second sequence we acknowledge debt to Master Balzac. I myself shall be king. (*Walking to the throne.*) It is a court of grievance. A crowd of courtiers, etcetera. It is my morning to dispense justice. I, you will note, am very kinglike. Observe my walk, my grace, how the very air around me is scented with power and authority. See how they bow, even cringe. Their positions, their wealth, their lives are in my hands. They *know* that I am sometimes given to *whim*, that I can be *capricious*, that even though the air they breathe is heavy with the finest scents of the Orient, there is danger, too. For I am king. *I am king.* And all know that I am king.

(*He laughs as he sits. They bow. A* YOUNG MAN *is brought in struggling. Gasps from the court, muffled cries of "No! No!" from the women, and excited whispers. The guards force him to his knees and gag him. An ugly old man, followed by his weeping daughter, steps forward and bows low.*)

Silence! (*Instant silence.*) You may speak, my loyal Duke.

(*The* YOUNG MAN *protests during the* DUKE's *speech, but because gagged he cannot be understood.*)

DUKE: Most Gracious Majesty, this pretender to wealth and name insinuated himself into my household under the pretext of seeking my daughter's hand. I welcomed him, treated him like a son. We hunted together, we drank the good wine of Burgundy, I confided in him, I left him in anterooms to whisper sweet nothings to my only daughter. And what do I discover? Why, that the man is low-born, a penniless student, and an imposter. That he has come to steal my money and my gold plate. That he has abused my hospitality and compromised the good name of my daughter. That, Sire, is what I have discovered.

MA-GICO: Ho-hum. And what does the accused have to say to all this? (*The* YOUNG MAN *gives an impassioned speech but cannot be understood.*)

Hang him.

(*The* YOUNG MAN *lets out pitiful groans as the rope is put around his neck.*)

Let him speak his final words.

(*The gag is removed. He coughs.*)

YOUNG MAN: I—

(*He can say no more for they hang him. He twists and kicks, gets a huge erection, and dies. The* DUKE's *daughter faints.*)

MA-GICO: Let justice be served. Always.

(*The court bows. An ugly old* WIDOW *approaches the* YOUNG MAN *slowly, sees the erection, and cackles with delight. She cannot resist touching it. As she speaks to the* KING, *she tugs at it and plays with it, cackling with distraction.*)

WIDOW: Your majesty, my husband, when he lived, served you faithfully.
MA-GICO: True:
WIDOW He fought in your wars, brought riches to your treasury, and followed you loyally at Court.
MA-GICO: True. What is your wish?
WIDOW: This young man. Give him to me. I shall see that he is properly buried—after a decent interval. (*The court laughs.*) It is a small request, your Majesty.
MA-GICO: I think it is a *large* request, rather.

(*The* WIDOW *cackles loudly, shaking the erection.*)

WIDOW: Aye! Aye! Large enough for an old woman like me!
MA-GICO: What say you, Courtiers?
MEN: (*Laughing*) Yes. . . .
WOMEN: No. . . .
MA-GICO: So be it. He is yours, my faithful widow, in recompense for your husband's many years of service.
WIDOW: (*Shaking the erection and cackling*) Bless you! Bless you, Sire!

(*The* YOUNG MAN *groans.*)

THE COURT: He lives! A miracle! She has revived him!

(*The* widow's *joy is uncontainable.*)

DUKE: Your Majesty, you must hang him again!

(*His daughter swoons.*)

WIDOW: No, no! You have given your royal word! He is mine! (*Shaking his erection and cackling*) Mine!

MA-GICO: So be it. I have given my word. But I shall make him truly yours. Stand him up properly. Bring him here. Do you, Widow Fiquis, take this man to be your husband?

WIDOW: (*Cackling*) I do!

MA-GICO: And do you, Monsieur— (*To* DUKE.) What is his name?

DUKE: Roulade.

MA-GICO: —Monsieur Roulade, take the Widow Fiquis to be your wife?

YOUNG MAN: (*Still dazed, but aware of what is happening and about to protest*) I— (*The rope is tightened. He gags.*) I do! I do!

(*The* DUKE's *daughter swoons.*)

MA-GICO: Then I declare you, forever, man and wife!

(*Shouts, cheers. Music. A stately walk around the chamber, led by the* KING. *Courtiers carry the* DUKE's *daughter. The* WIDOW *leads the* YOUNG MAN *by his now dwindling leash.*)

And so, justice again triumphs. The Duke's daughter is saved from a penniless interloper, the Widow Fiquis is made happy in her declining years, a young man receives a second life, and wealth in the bargain, and the good people of my court are entertained for a day. God is truly bountiful.

THE COURT: *Vive le roi! Vive le roi! Vive le roi!*

(*The walk ends. They sit.* MA-GICO *center stage.*)

MA-GICO: I make a lovely king, don't you think? But a better magician. You must not forget that. I am a magician. *Dr. Ma-Gico!* Say it to yourselves and see if there isn't magic in the name itself. *Ma-Gico! Ma-Gico! Master magician!* (*He laughs quickly.*) And why? Let me give you hints. I am not a prestidigitator. I do *not* deal in tricks. (*He pulls a flower out of a handkerchief.*) Only fools deal in tricks. I deal in life. My mysteries do not come out of a hat. See in this next sequence if you can find the magic. —And look for the theme— Is the magic in the mystery or is the mystery in the magic? (*He laughs.*) —And say to yourself, over and over, always, *Ma-Gico! Ma-Gico! Dr. Ma-Gico!* as the scene unfolds. (*He swings his cape.*) Music! Gypsies!

(*Tambourines and drums. In the distance, a church bell ringing, which continues throughout the scene, its volume increasing finally to head-splitting intensity.*)

These people are the gypsies of the streets of Paris! It is night! In the shadows, the beggars, the deformed, the diseased of the Western world! The gypsies dance! And those in shadow look on hungrily! Suddenly, a confusion, a babbling of voices, and Quasimoda, lumbering like an ape, leaps into their midst! What a grotesque sight he is! An eruption of nightmare! The music stops! The gypsies stare! Quasimoda is panting! He is covered with sweat and dust! With a tongue swollen in his mouth, the words like hot coals, he speaks, thickly, longingly, painfully— (QUASIMODA *does not speak.* MA-GICO *whips him with his wand.*) Speak! Speak now!

QUASIMODA: (*After a pause, slowly, looking around with animal-frightened eyes, then staring at the audience, an eerie, unearthly, terrifying voice, a cry of pain.*) *Eth-mer-alda! Eth-mer-alda! Eth-mer-alda!* (*Howling.*) *Eth-mer-aldaaa!*

(*A long silence.*)

MA-GICO: They are silent. The gypsies do not know what to make of the hunchback who cannot hear his own grotesque voice. They do not know what to make of this babble of passion. Finally, perhaps out of fear, they laugh, at first timidly, then with confidence. And while they are laughing, the beautiful Esmeralda comes running into their midst.

QUASIMODA: *Eth-mer-aldaaa!*

MA-GICO: She screams. She is face to face with the thing she most fears. Listen. Listen to her scream.

QUASIMODA: (*As she is screaming*) *Eth-mer-aldaaa! Eth-mer-aldaaa!*

MA-GICO: Quasimoda lunges suddenly toward her. But the gypsies interfere, holding Quasimoda back. Come, come, they say to her; if you can dance, you can be one of us, we shall save you. (*Walking to* ESMERALDA.) Do you hear, Esmeralda? If you can dance, they will save you. So dance! (*He rips off her dress.*) Dance! Dance for your life!

(*Music.* ESMERALDA *dances, faster and faster.*)

QUASIMODA: (*As she dances*) *Eth-mer-aldaaa!*

MA-GICO: And so, Esmeralda dances. The gypsies watch. Quasimoda calls out, but in vain. And those in the shadows creep closer. The ugly, the diseased, the deformed creep closer to the beauty that is Esmeralda. Her radiance shines through the night that is Paris, and the shadows reach *out* to her. Be careful, be careful. Look behind you, gypsies. No, no, no! —It is too late! They swarm over her with their festering sores and their crutches and their stumps, feasting on her beauty, crazed with longing and pain. And Quasimoda—

QUASIMODA: *Eth-mer-aldaaa!*

MA-GICO: He cannot move. Esmeralda screams—once—and it is over. The shadows suck back their own. The gypsies huddle together by their fire in confusion and fear, their song, their dance, dead for the night, perhaps forever. On the ground, white and still, Esmeralda, who was beauty. Esmeralda who was life and joy. Esmeralda who was loved by Quasimoda. He rises, hobbles slowly to her side, picks her

Kenneth Bernard

up tenderly, bends to kiss her, cannot, *cannot violate her even in death!*, and cries, weeps, moans, howls.

QUASIMODA: (*As the lights fade*) Eth-mer-aldaaa! Eth-mer-aldaaa! . . .

MA-GICO: She is dead! Esmeralda is dead!

(*He laughs, as the church bell becomes unbearable and there is total darkness. Then, after a pause, bright lights and music. A minuet. The minuet ends.*)

Wait. Another turn, I think.

(*They dance again, then take their seats.*)

Yes, That's better. —What were we talking about? Yes, magic. (*He pulls an egg out of the air.*) So simple, is it not? For children. Infants! —*I eat infants!* (*He laughs.*) I shall sit during this episode. I find the passions tiring, so very tiring. (*He sits.*) Ahh. Ma-Gico's throne. This is Ma-Gico's throne. From here I control all. Do you not feel the strings? But it isn't the throne, really. It's my voice. And my eyes, my beautiful and penetrating eyes. They are convincing, my voice and my eyes, very convincing. My voice is deep and resonant. *Resonnante.* I speak French beautifully. (*Loudly.*) *Voulez vous coucher avec moi?* (*He laughs.*) Italian, too, but it is too frivolous so I rarely speak it.—*Momento! Avanti! Basta, basta!* You see? Ma-Gico knows it all (*He laughs.*) Now this episode must be watched closely. It is a thing of the head and the eyes. And ears, too. It is intriguing rather than gripping, mystifying rather than frightening. And the mirrors, watch the mirrors. Every eye is a mirror. These people before me. (*He snaps his fingers.*) You two over there. Come. They are lovers. His name is Jacques, her name is Marie. (*He snaps his fingers again.*) Animate! Animate! (*Italian.*) *Animate!*

JACQUES: I love you.

MARIE: *I* love *you.*

JACQUES: I love you more than life itself.

MARIE: *Liar.* Liar, first of all. And second, what good would you be to me dead?

JACQUES: It's true. (*Handing her a knife.*) Put me to the test, if you dare.

MARIE: You mean, ask you to prove yourself by killing yourself?

JACQUES: Yes.

(MARIE *laughs.*)

MARIE: I'll give you another test instead. Here. Cut off your jewels.* Now. At once. (*He does not take the knife and she laughs loudly. He is shamed.*) Oh, no, no, no, don't fret, my brave little cock. I understand. But you must grow up a little. Men make the best lovers. Always. Now, listen. Listen carefully. Go away and come right back. When you return, I shall be disguised as another woman. I want you to make love to that women. Truly. You must not recognize me. If you do, I shall never be your wife. You must woo the other woman that I am until you win her love. Completely. And you must never reproach me for anything she says or does. Understood? This is your test.

JACQUES: (*Laughing*) Understood. I'll go at once.

(*He skips off, delighted at the new game.* MARIE *goes behind the mirrors and comes out veiled and disguised as an ugly old woman.* JACQUES *returns. She turns to him and drops her veil. She is repulsive.* JACQUES *is shocked. He cannot believe that this toad is his* MARIE.)

OLD WOMAN: Well? What do you want? What are you staring at?

JACQUES: I—I want to be your lover.

(*She laughs hideously.*)

OLD WOMAN: Oh, you do, do you? I have very special requirements and tastes, as befitting my age and condition.

---

*I.e., testicles.

Kenneth Bernard

JACQUES: I'll—I'll try to meet them. I have long worshiped you from afar, but dared not speak— (*She laughs.*) lest I—I—

OLD WOMAN: I'll bet. (*She laughs.*) Worshiped from afar, eh?

JACQUES: (*Kneeling*) Please tell me that I may love you. I adore you. I'll do anything you say.

OLD WOMAN: Do you know about my sores?

JACQUES: Sores?

OLD WOMAN: Yes. *My sores.* (*Touching herself sensually.*) On my body. All around, and within my . . . *orifices.* —Are you afraid?

JACQUES: No!

OLD WOMAN: Repelled?

JACQUES: No!

OLD WOMAN: They suppurate.

JACQUES: What?

OLD WOMAN: They *ooze pus.* — Does that make you hesitate?

JACQUES: (*After a pause*) No!

OLD WOMAN: Kiss me, then! Kiss me, my young lover!

JACQUES: Kiss you?

OLD WOMAN: Yes, Kiss me. On the mouth. Hold your nose, if you wish. Come. Come. (*He kisses her tepidly.*) No, no, you fool! With your tongue! I want your tongue resting on my own so I may *suck* on it for the juices. Can you kiss that way? You've done it before, haven't you? You're not *that* young, are you?

JACQUES: Yes. . . . Yes, I've done it, but—

OLD WOMAN: (*Screeching*) Then *do* it! (*He hesitates.*) Do it!

(*He does, then struggles back with a scream, as she shrieks laughter. There is blood on his lips.*)

JACQUES: (*Gagging, almost unable to speak*) You . . . you *bit* it! You *bit* my tongue!

OLD WOMAN: And I'll *get* it next time.

JACQUES: No.

OLD WOMAN: (*Coquettishly*) You don't love me anymore?

JACQUES: Yes! Yes, I do.

The Magic Show of Dr. Ma-Gico 173

OLD WOMAN: Then make love to me.

JACQUES: I—I want to make love in another way.

OLD WOMAN: What way? (*Pause, slow smile.*) With my . . . *orifice?*

JACQUES: Yes. With your orifice.

OLD WOMAN: But I don't *like* anything in *that* orifice.

JACQUES: Why not? What do you mean?

OLD WOMAN: It *hurts* me. It's too *diseased*. (*She laughs.*) You're worried? —Oh, no, no, the other one's diseased, too, lucky for you. (*Pause.*) There's only one left, isn't there? (*She smiles, thrusting her rotten teeth at him.*) Yes, yes, this one. You can put it there. It's the only way I care to do it anymore. Do you understand?

JACQUES: I think so.

OLD WOMAN: (*Shrieking laughter*) You think so, you think so! Like a schoolboy! I want to eat you, to put it in my *mouth*. Do you get the picture? It's my best orifice these days. (*She laughs.*)

JACQUES: (*Without conviction*) You have lovely lips. I adore you.

OLD WOMAN: (*Screeching laughter*) Correct! correct! I have lovely lips, and you adore me. You haven't mentioned my nipples yet.

JACQUES: Your—?

OLD WOMAN: (*Screeching laughter again*) Never mind, never mind. Let my nipples be. Let sleeping dugs lie. (*She laughs.*) Lie down. (*He hesitates. She screams.*) Lie down, you young fool! Lie down, I say! It isn't every day I have a lover, a man who *adores* me.

(*He lies down. She takes out a rope.*)

JACQUES What's that? What are you doing?

OLD WOMAN: Oh, I've got to tie you. I can't enjoy it unless you're *help-less*. (*Tying him.*) It makes no difference, you know. Same orifice, tied or not. Tell me again that you love me.

JACQUES: I love you.

OLD WOMAN: Do you truly?

JACQUES: Yes.

OLD WOMAN: (*Carefully*) *Would you die for me?*

JACQUES: Yes.

OLD WOMAN: Do you mean it?

JACQUES: (*Angrily*) Yes! Get on with it!

OLD WOMAN: (*Laughing*) Oh, temper, temper, now. (*She opens his pants.*) Oh, that's lovely. —Now do you know what I'm going to do to you?

JACQUES: Yes.

OLD WOMAN: What?

JACQUES: Put it in your mouth. Eat it.

OLD WOMAN: *Yes.* You've got it exactly. I didn't get your tongue, but I'm going to get your *cock.* (*She shows her teeth.*) I told you it was the only way I could *do* it.

JACQUES: (*Struggling, as it dawns on him what she really means*) No! No! Marie, no! don't do it! No! . . .

(*He screams hideously as she bites off his penis, then rises, grunting orgasmically, with the bloody stump in her mouth, and staggers behind the mirrors.* MARIE *comes out, blood on her mouth, holding the veil. She kneels by* JACQUES *who groans pitifully and whose body jerks convulsively from the pain, the shock, the loss. She does not look at him.*)

MARIE: Jacques? Jacques? (*She touches him, but still does not look at him.*) Oh, Jacques, did you really mean it when you said you would die for me? (*She laughs.*) Jacques, you shouldn't have said "Marie." (*Shouting.*) I love you. Jacques! (*Blood spills out of her mouth.*)

(*A few moments of* JACQUES' *agony, then* MA-GICO *claps his hands sharply.*)

MA-GICO: Tarantella! Tarantella!

(*Lights out, then full. Everyone does the tarantella, after which* MA-GICO *takes stage center.*)

A poetic diversion. First, a poem of Poe, Edgar Allan, who came, as you know, to a very bad end.

(*Clearing his throat, very rhetorically.*)

Take this kiss upon the brow!
And, in parting from you now,
Thus much let me avow—
You are not wrong, who deem
That my days have been a dream;
Yet if hope has flown away
In a night, or in a day,
In a vision, or in none,
Is it therefore the less *gone?*
All that we see or seem
Is but a dream within a dream.

(*Pause. He clears his throat again.*)
Stanza two:

I stand amid the roar
Of a surf tormented shore,
And I hold within my hand
Grains of the golden sand—
How few! yet how they creep
Through my fingers to the deep,
While I weep—while I weep!
O God! can I not grasp
Them with a tighter clasp?
O God! can I not save
One from the pitiless wave?
Is *all* that we see or seem
But a dream within a dream?

(*Pause.*)

And then the Roman poet wrote:

(*Declaiming.*)

Non ignara mali miseris succurrere disco.
"Not unacquainted with suffering, I know how to give comfort to those
who suffer." The magnificent and tragic Dido, who loved only too well,
and burned on her own passion. (*Imitating* QUASIMODA.) *Eth-mer-aldaaa!*

(*He laughs as* ESMERALDA *joins him, and he recites the following poem
to her.**)

> J'aimais surtout ses jolis yeux,
> Plus clairs que l'étoile des cieux,
> J'aimais ses yeux malicieux.
>> Dansons la gigue!
> Elle avait des facons vraiment
> De desoler un pauvre amant,
>> Que c'en était vraiment charmant!
>> Dansons la gigue!
> Mais je trouve encor meilleur
> Le baiser de sa bouche en fleur,

(*He kisses her lips lightly.*)

> Depuis qu'elle est morte à mon coeur.
>> Dansons la gigue!
> Je me souviens, je me souviens
> Des heures et des entretiens,
> Et c'est le meilleur de mes biens.
>> Dansons la gigue!

(*Music. They dance a jig together. In the middle of it, he signals to the
servants, etc.*)

Encore!

---

*Verlaine, "Dansons la Gigue!" See end of play for translation.

(*They do a country dance, strong and awkward, sometimes a grotesque parody.* MA-GICO *and* ESMERALDA *finish, after which he seats her and bows.*)

Let's call that an interlude. Now comes the fairy tale, which we begin in the middle. *In media res.* It is night, and the moon shines brightly. Try to see the scene. *It is night, and the moon shines brightly.* Suddenly, there is music. It is the music of the dance, of the ballet, the music of beauty and white tutus and slender arms waving effortlessly. Across the moonbeams dances a young and beautiful princess—wait, she will appear—But she is enchanted. Her face, her body, they are ugly. (*She appears, dancing. She is grotesque.*) You see, I do not deceive you. She is ugly. Who could love that face? Who could lie next to that body? caress it? enfold oneself in it? She is almost totally without charm—but note the almost. She is, as I say, *enchanted.*

DANCER: (*In a gruff, flat voice, as she dances*) Where is my prince? Where is my prince?

MA-GICO: You will observe that she dances beautifully. See how she quivers, note the delicacy of her toes. For five long years now she has been enchanted, and each night that the moon shines brightly, she dances across this woodland glade and bemoans her fate.

DANCER: Where is my prince? Where is my prince?

MA-GICO: And then she folds up like a flower and goes to sleep. Her father, the king (*he is carried out on a chair*), has grown old and wizened lamenting his daughter, whom he loved dearly. He is senile. He slobbers. His wife is dead. His courtiers mock him. Only his daughter can dry his tears. And she, like so many of us, is *enchanted.* (*Music. She dances again.*) Yes, King, she is *enchanted.* Do you know that she is *enchanted?* (*He slaps the* KING.) King! Do you know that your daughter is enchanted?

DANCER: My prince! Where is my prince?

MA-GICO: He is deaf also. He cannot hear her. He cannot hear anything. But his eyes look for her. See? See? She dances in front of him and he does not see her. He does not see his daughter, who is *enchant-ed*. (*Slapping him.*) King! What is it you miss? What do you regret? What pains you in your old and dying heart?—Is it your silken sheets? The soothing hand of your dead wife? The soft and softly curls of your golden child? Her trusting hand warmly in yours? (*Slapping him.*) What is it, King? Wake up! What have you lost? Why does the sun no longer shine for you? Speak! Speak!

KING: (*Slowly, with great difficulty*) Fwog!

MA-GICO: (*Slapping him*) What? Speak up!

KING; Fwog! Fwog!

MA-GICO: Ah yes. Frog. A new element. He says frog. It is night, and the moon shines brightly. The old king says frog. Somewhere in this tale there is a frog. But where? Is the frog evil? Is the frog good? Will a frog one day come and break the enchantment? And if so, who is the frog? King! King! Do you know? (*Slapping him.*) King!

KING: Fwog! Fwog!

MA-GICO: See how he slobbers it. He does not even remember the witch whom once he offended. Do not pity him. Once he was rich and pow-erful and gloried in both. He was vain and sometimes cruel.—But he loved his daughter truly. And she was lovely. (*Music. She dances.*) With her he was tender, with her he was kind. His heart, in her pres-ence, was soft and beautiful.

DANCER: Where is my prince? Where is my prince?

KING: (*Looking at her*) Fwog! . . . Fwog! . . .

(*A Prince enters.*)

MA-GICO: Ahhh! And there he is, rather late, the Prince. Handsome, strong, good, and in love. But with whom? Yes, with whom? The fat and ugly dancer of the night? Or the old and slobbering king? Which one is his enchanted princess? He does not know. His instructions are simple. He must kill one to save the other. But which? Which shall he kill? Which shall he save?

DANCER: Where is my prince?—Where is my prince?

KING: Fwog! Fwog!

MA-GICO: He is undecided, but twelve bells will ring and he must act then or lose his chance forever.

(*Bells.*)

DANCER: My prince! Where is my prince?
MA-GICO: Oh, my princess, he thinks, and rushes to her with open arms.
KING: (*Urgently*) Fwog! Fwog!
MA-GICO: He turns. Is *that* his princess? No, no, it cannot be! That old and ugly thing cannot be his princess. He draws his sword.—Quick, quick, the twelfth bell, you fool!

(*He turns and pierces the* DANCER'S *throat.*)

DANCER: My prin—!
MA-GICO: And she falls. Then, slowly, he approaches the king. His princess, he thinks. The King looks, and sees the fallen dancer. And although she is still fat and ugly, somehow he knows now that it is his daughter, his soft and beautiful daughter, whom he once cuddled in his lap, a small, living, loving thing. And as the Prince kneels, kisses his hands, his neck, his lips in search of metamorphosis, the King weeps, his heart breaks, and he dies. The Prince is left alone.— He has killed the wrong one! He sits on the King's chair. He says nothing. He becomes very still. Prince! Why don't you speak? (*Slapping him.*) Prince! Prince! Speak! Speak up!
PRINCE: *Fwog!* . . . *Fwog!* . . . *Fwog!* . . .

(*Music. The* DANCER *rises and dances as she speaks.*)

DANCER: Where is my prince? Where is my prince? . . .

(*The lights fade to blackout, then full lights. They all dance a saraband, after which* MA-GICO, *stage front.*)

MA-GICO: I really think we've had enough of kings for a while. And where are the queens, you ask? Equal time? Well, I don't know. Maybe later. Queens don't seem as interesting somehow.—Any queens out there? Queens with magical stories? Something like "The Queen's Garter" or "The Queen Who Wouldn't Go to Bed"?

VOICE: Do it!

MA-GICO: Never. Much too frivolous. Besides, we have room for only two more episodes, one for coherence and one for a dramatic curtain.—Watch this. (*He pulls a flower out of his hand.*) What we need for the next episode is an image. No, a metaphor. True magic is metaphor. *The babe that wets the flower. The lion silent and still by the sleeping gypsy, 'neath the moon. O gypsy love! O gypsy! Wild on the shores of my throbbing heart!*—Watch this. (*He pulls a coin out of the air.*) Yes, let us have a *gypsy!* (*A dark and beautiful gypsy runs out. Castanets.*) And . . . yes, a procession. Why not? A royal procession. (*The castanets stop. Royal music. A procession.*)—With King, Queen—yes, there's your queen—noblemen and noble ladies, their lackeys, dogs, jugglers, tumblers, servants, dwarfs, fools, beggars, and lepers. Come, come, around the arena, my Lords and Ladies! . . . More volume! . . . March! . . . One and all, march! . . . And now, quickly, the gypsy girl! Castanets!

(*She enters. The music stops, the procession halts.*)

QUEEN: Who is that strange creature, my Lord?

KING: Riffraff. A girl of the streets.

QUEEN: What does she want?

KING: What does any beggar want—money!

(*He laughs and throws her coins. She spits on them, then steps in front of the procession and quivers to the sound of the castanets.*)

QUEEN: My Lord, she has insulted you. What does she want?

GYPSY GIRL: (*Laughing*) Peeg!

KING: Remove her!

QUEEN: My Lord, she should pay with her life.

KING: (*After a pause*) Remove her, I say!

(*Several from his entourage remove her.*)

GYPSY GIRL: (*Struggling and laughing*) Peeg! . . . Peeg! . . .

KING: Continue the procession! Forward!

(*Music. The procession leaves. Lights down.*)

MA-GICO: (*Flitting across the stage*) The bed chamber of the king and queen that night.

QUEEN: My Lord, you are very silent.

KING: I am very silent.

QUEEN: *Why* are you very silent?

KING: Why?

(*Castanets. The* KING *stands poised. Then he taps his foot and claps his hands to the rhythm of the castanets.*)

QUEEN: My Lord!

(*The castanets stop.*)

KING: Yes, my queen?

QUEEN: It has been . . . a long time since you . . . fulfilled your marriage duties.

KING: Yes. I am getting old.

QUEEN: Old?

KING: Yes. Did you not notice today?

QUEEN: Today?

KING: The *gypsy.*

(*Castanets. He raises his hands and dances.*)

QUEEN: My Lord! What about the gypsy? (*He does not answer.*) My Lord!

(*The castanets cease. The* KING *stops dancing, looks at the* QUEEN *with a private smile.*)

KING: Yes, I am very silent tonight. I am getting old.

QUEEN: (*Taking off her dress. Urgently*) My Lord, it has been a long time since you performed your kindly duty! I . . . I am your faithful queen.

KING: (*Taking her breasts in his hands*) Your breasts have always out-shone the moon in beauty. But your nipples are large and dark, and the moon is pale.

QUEEN: Yes, my Lord. It is true.

KING: And I have lusted for the moon, to feel it twixt my lips! To bite into its mystery!

(*He kisses her breast roughly.*)

QUEEN: My Lord? More gently. I am not the moon.

(*She rubs his head.*)

KING: Your nipples are large and dark!

QUEEN: Yes, my Lord. And hard as just-ripe plums for the plucking.

(*Castanets. The* KING *rises and listens.*)

My Lord!

(*He dances again. She removes her shift.*)

My Lord! My nipples are large and dark! They are hard as just-ripe plums for the plucking!

KING: I cannot hear you! I am getting old!

(*She removes the covering of her breasts and squeezes them.*)

QUEEN: My Lord! I am not the moon! (*The castanets stop. The* KING *looks at her.*) But my nipples are large and dark, and hard as just-ripe plums for the plucking!

(*She removes her last garment.*)

And here, here between my legs, there is heat. Heat, my Lord, to warm you on your journey, your kingly journey. (*She lies on the bed, spreads and bends her legs, undulates.*) My Lord! Your coach is ready! (*He goes to the bed, opens his robe, and lies on her.*) Oh, my Lord, how *hungry* I am! Fill me! Fill me!

(*Castanets. The* KING'S *movements become more intense, then violent.*)

My Lord! (*Urgently.*) My Lord! You go too far!—Ah! Ah! Ahh! My Lord, cease! Desist!—Ahhhhh!—My Lord! (*She screams.*)
KING: (*As she screams*) I seek the moon!

(*Loud pounding without. The castanets are muted.*)

VOICE: My Lord! My Lord! Is all well?
KING: (*Rising from the inert* QUEEN) Yes. . . . All is well.

(*He walks to the center of the room as the castanets come up again. He dances, at first with confinement, then with greater and greater force and abandonment as the lights fade.*)

(*Lights,* MA-GICO *leaping onstage.*)

MA-GICO: Time for *my* solo now. I don't want to be shown up by a mere king, you know. And don't take those castanets too seriously.

(*He snaps his fingers. Music, a graceful villanella. He dances well, sometimes intricately, always with refinement. At particularly fine turns, some oohs and ahhs, occasional small bursts of applause. When he is done, genteel applause.*)

Thank you, thank you. (*Wiping his brow.*) Thank you. I love the dance. . . . I am hearing it always, wherever I go, whatever I do. My head swims with it. My heart is always keeping time. And it's getting late, dear friends, late.

VOICES: (*Politely*) No. No. . . .

MA-GICO: Yes. It's getting late. Soon the hobgoblins will be out. And you must all be safely in your nests. For our finale, which is really too grandiose a term, we come back to our king. Did he die or didn't he? I forget. At any rate, he is king again. He holds his scepter and his sphere. His crown still rests precariously on his head. But he is blind. *The king is blind.* (*The* KING *gropes his way to the throne.*) How did he *get* blind? I don't know. It doesn't really matter. Of course, whenever he moves he is terribly awkward and unkingly. He stumbles, drops his crown sometimes, crawls, walks into things. He is quite laughable. Just look at him. Pitiful and grotesque. *But* . . . once he gains his throne, scrambles like a frightened rat into it, he feels secure. He arranges himself like a king, and, though blind as a bat, stares out into nothingness with confidence and serenity. Tonight, as every night, he will be assassinated. But it will not be easy. You see, his hearing is very sharp. And once he hears his assassin, he cannot be killed, for he is king and he sits on his throne. Of course, if he ever acts as if he *isn't* blind, actually *sees* anybody, then he will be killed instantly, for he is a *blind king.* That is his state and condition. Let me illustrate. In the background is a *knave.* He has been beaten within an inch of his life for something he did not do. He seeks revenge. See how he creeps up on the king from behind. See the glint of his knife. See the knave with his shining knife as he sneaks up on the blind king.

(*As the* KNAVE *creeps closer, the* KING*'s ears are alert, but he is not sure. Suddenly, the* KNAVE *stumbles on the platform of the throne.*)

KING: (*Shrieking*) Seize him! Seize him!

(GUARDS *rush in and drag the* KNAVE *away.*)

MA-GICO: And now the king is alone again. The knave will have his head cut off. What thoughts does the king have? Why does he smile? What creatures inhabit his dark world? —Shhh. A courtier has entered. He is about to speak when he sees that he and the king are alone. Now is his chance. For he hates the king, who has debauched his lady. He loosens the cord around his waist and makes a noose. Slowly, carefully, he inches forward. The king is alert, but hears nothing. Several times it seems as if the courtier will lose his balance, but he doesn't. And then—Shhh.

(*Silence. The sound of the* COURTIER*'s slipper sliding on the floor.*)

KING: (*Addressing him*) My Lord! (*No answer.*) I said, my Lord! Speak!
COURTIER: I—I seek the Lady Eleanor. I seek my Lady Eleanor.
MA-GICO: The king laughs. The courtier backs out awkwardly. He knows the king will have him castrated, or his eyes put out, or his hands chopped off. Escape is impossible. He is doomed. The king knows why the courtier did not address him at once. And that is why he laughs. He rejoices in his strength and power. But soon it is quiet again. The king becomes bored. He sings to while away the time.
KING: (*Singing*)

> The birds of the spring
> Are coming to bring
> O joy, O joy, my joy!

MA-GICO: But he has no voice, so he stops. He yawns, he scratches, he listens. —Nothing. Then he appears to nap. The Lady Eleanor enters.

She has heard the bad news. But she does not come to beg mercy for her lover. (*She takes out a knife.*) No. She comes for revenge. She comes to kill the king. She gets closer than anyone yet on this day. —But not close enough, for the king's nose warns him. He sniffs. He smells the perfumes of the Lady Eleanor.

KING: (*Half-rising*) Be gone! . . . Be gone! . . .

MA-GICO: She is petrified. She cannot move.

KING: (*Fiercely*) Be gone, I say!

MA-GICO The Lady Eleanor faints. She drops her knife. The king laughs. (*Picking up the knife.*) What a sharp and wicked little weapon it is, a woman's weapon. (*He makes a little cut in the air and strolls behind the* KING.) She has courage, the Lady Eleanor. And the king will not have her killed, for he still lusts after her. Even more now, for the taking will be sweeter. The king relaxes. He wonders whether the day is over, who else may come, when he can eat, when rest, when sleep. (MA-GICO *puts the knife by the* KING's *throat.*) Three attempts today, and still he is king, just as he has been king for many days, weeks, months. How long has it been? He can't remember, but long, a long time. And he laughs. He laughs because he had been king a long time. (MA-GICO *slowly slits the* KING's *throat. Blood. The* KING *looks surprised, gags, dies.*) Perhaps he has been king too long. No matter. He is king no longer. His throat is slit. (*He chuckles.*) Yes, the throat of the blind king is slit. (*He laughs more and throws down the knife.*) The throat of the blind king is slit! (He laughs loudly.)

(*Music. A minuet. Slow and stately. All except the* KING. *The music stops several times and, as the lights go out, a single spot on one of the dancers, who utters—deeply, grotesquely, painfully— "Eth-mer-al-daaa!" or "Fwog!" Finally, a single spot on* MA-GICO.)

MA-GICO: (*Throwing a few kisses into the darkness as he speaks softly*) Good night. Good night. Good night.

(*Spot out.*)

END

Verlaine's "Let's Dance the Jig"

More than anything I loved her pretty eyes,
clearer than the stars in the skies,
but very malicious.
   Let's dance the jig!
And she had a way
that made her poor lovers despair,
yet was wickedly delicious.
   Let's dance the jig!
But I remember even more
the kiss of her flower mouth—
especially since I've lost her.
   Let's dance the jig!
And I remember, I remember
little talks and intimacies
which are the best of all my goods.
   Let's dance the jig!

Library of Congress Cataloging-in-Publication Data

Theatre of the ridiculous / [edited by Bonnie Marranca, Gautam Dasgupta].—
Rev. ed.
    p.   cm.
    Contents: Preface to the 1998 edition—Introduction to the 1979 edition /
Bonnie Marranca—The theatre of Jack Smith / J. Hoberman—Rehearsal for the
destruction of Atlantis / Jack Smith—The plays of Ronald Tavel / Bonnie Marran-
ca—The life of Lady Godiva / Ronald Tavel—Theatre and the ridiculous / Gautam
Dasgupta—Stage bood / Charles Ludlam—Kenneth Bernard and John Vaccaro /
Gerald Rabkin—The magic show of Dr. Ma-Gico / Kenneth Bernard.
    ISBN 0-8018-5697-3 (h : alk. paper).—ISBN 0-8018-5698-1 (pbk. : alk.
paper).
    1. American drama—New York (State)—New York.   2. American drama—
20th century.   3. Ridiculous Theatrical Company.   I. Marranca, Bonnie.
II. Dasgupta, Gautam.   III. Smith, Jack, 1932–   IV. Tavel, Ronald. Life of lady Godiva.   V. Ludlam, Charles.
Stage blood.   VI. Bernard, Kenneth.   Magic show of Dr. Ma-Gico.
Rehearsal for the destruction
of Atlantis.
    PS549.N5T47   1998
    812'.50917—dc21

97-15815
CIP